HOW TO THINK CLEARLY AGAIN

WHEN REPEATED LIES FEEL TRUE

The Simple Psychology Of How Smart People Believe Manipulative Propaganda

W. B. Hazel

THANK YOU

THANK YOU FOR PURCHASING MY BOOK! LIKE IT? PLEASE LET ME KNOW. I LOVE YOUR REVIEWS. PLEASE RATE AND REVIEW THIS BOOK TO HELP MY BUSINESS GROW.

SCAN THE QR CODE
LEAVE YOUR AMAZON REVIEW!

Paperback ISBN: 979-8-9955915-1-1
Cover design by W. B. Hazel, photo from Pixabay
Photos for Intro, ch 1-11 and Bonus design by W. B. Hazel via Chat GPT
Photo for ch 12 by W. B. Hazel
Editing and Guidance by Mat Ward and Profitable Publisher 3.0/Barry KDP
fishingfrogprinthouse@gmail.com

TABLE OF CONTENTS

CONTENTS

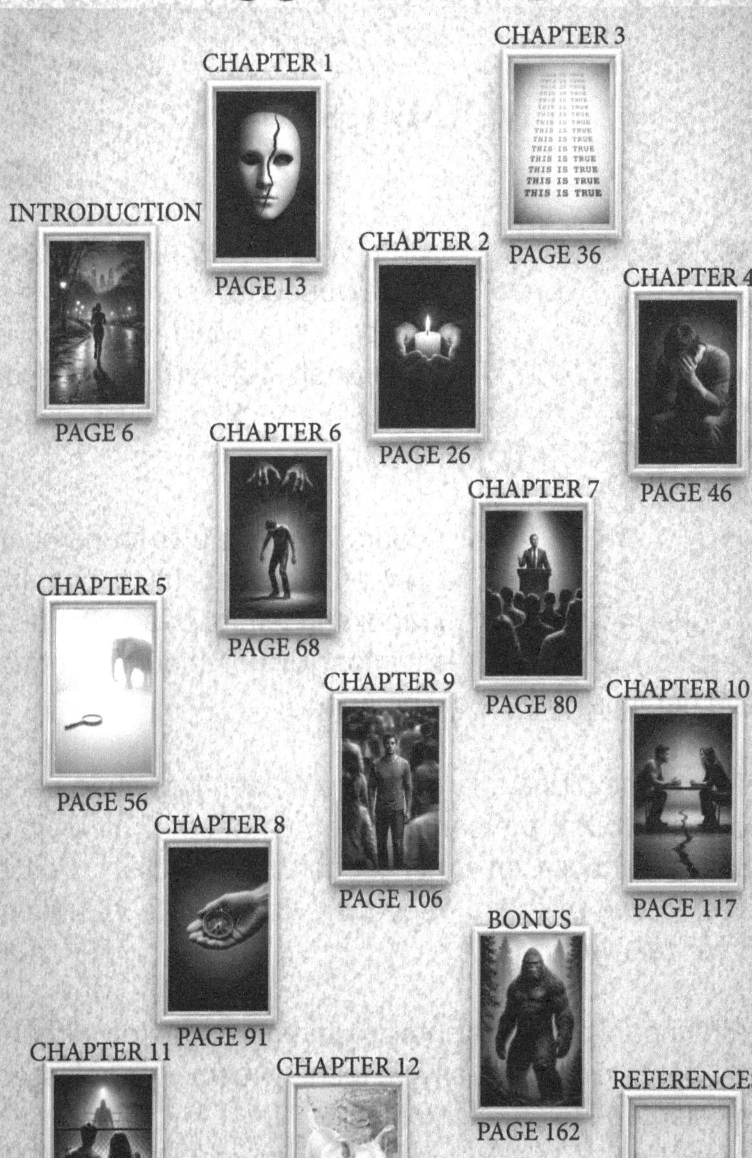

INTRODUCTION

Five Confessions

On a Wednesday night in April 1989, a young investment banker named Trisha Meili went for a jog through the northern end of Central Park. She never came home.

Hours later, she was found near a ravine. She had been beaten, bound, and left for dead. She had lost most of her blood. Doctors gave her little chance of survival.

That same night, a large group of teenagers had been moving through the park. Some had been involved in a series of attacks on other joggers and cyclists. Police arrested five of them. They were only fourteen, fifteen, and sixteen years old.

After hours of lengthy interrogations conducted without their parents present, all five teens eventually confessed on videotape to attacking Meili.[1]

The confessions were broadcast on news channels across the country. Newspapers ran the story as front page news. Polls showed the majority of New Yorkers considered the case closed. The five boys had confessed. What more was there to question?

Public anger grew quickly. A full page advertisement appeared in several major New York newspapers calling for the return of the death penalty.

But, something didn't fit.

There was no physical evidence connecting any of the five boys to the attack. No DNA match. No blood. No fibers. Nothing placed them at the scene.

The medical evidence indicated a single attacker. Investigators had collected a semen sample at the beginning of the investigation. That evidence did not match any of the five teenagers.[2]

All of this information was available at the time of trial.

However, the confessions had already shaped the story. Once that narrative was established, new evidence was filtered through it rather than judged against it.

All five of the teens were convicted. They served between six and thirteen years in prison. One boy was tried as an adult and sent to Rikers Island at the age of sixteen.

In 2002, a man named Matias Reyes came forward. He was already serving a life sentence for murder and multiple rapes. He confessed to attacking Trisha Meili alone.

His DNA matched the sample investigators had collected years earlier.

The convictions of all five men were vacated. New York City later settled a wrongful conviction lawsuit for forty one million dollars.[3]

Psychologists call part of what happened in this case anchoring.[4]

The jurors who convicted the Central Park Five believed they were impartial. In reality, the first story they heard had already shaped how they interpreted everything that followed. Later evidence did not replace the first story.

What makes anchoring dangerous is that it doesn't feel like you have a bias. It feels like reasoning.

Why Smart People Are Not Immune

The legal case eventually ended.

However, the debate wasn't settled for everyone.

Linda Fairstein led the Manhattan sex crimes unit that prosecuted the case. She was a well respected prosecutor who had spent her career building cases on evidence. Even after the DNA evidence proved the five men were innocent, she continued to maintain publicly that they had been involved in the attack.

She held that position for nearly two decades after the DNA evidence proved their innocence.

Linda was a smart woman who had reached a detailed, sound conclusion of what she thought happened in Central Park in 1989. It was an account she'd staked her professional reputation on.

Intelligence doesn't protect against this kind of reasoning. Research consistently shows it amplifies it.[5]

That story, the one that was repeated across news rooms, courtrooms, and public discussions felt solid and unquestionable to her. She encountered the false claim enough times that it stopped feeling like a claim and started feeling like something she'd always known.

Linda fell victim to a well documented phenomenon called the illusory truth effect.[6]

When contradictory evidence was presented, it collided with a story she already felt certain about. Linda's feeling of certainty was not a reliable signal of sound thinking.[7]

Officials who craft narratives, engineer information, and decide which facts get amplified and which get buried have studied this psychology carefully. By design, you are influenced everyday.

Governments, media organizations, political campaigns, and advocacy groups all operate in environments where attention and repetition count. They know the first story people hear often matters the most, and that repeated messages can slowly turn claims into acceptable facts.

The important question isn't whether you're vulnerable to these effects, everyone is. The real question is whether you understand how these mental processes work and what that knowledge allows us to do differently.

When I first began reading the research behind this book, I assumed it described other people. The most unsettling studies were not on gullibility or ignorance. They were about intelligence.

Realizing that changed how I read the news, and how I argued with people. Eventually it's what led me to write this book.

What This Book Is About And How To Read It

The jurors who convicted the Central Park Five had evidence, proving their innocence, right in front of them. They processed it through a framework so firmly set by the time they entered the jury room that contradictory facts registered not as reasons to doubt guilt, but as obstacles for them to explain away.

They weren't aware they were operating off of a bias. They thought they were doing the opposite: setting aside emotion, weighing the evidence, reaching a reasoned verdict.

The tendency to observe thinking errors in others while genuinely not knowing they are operating in yourself[8] is called a bias blind spot.

This applied to the jurors, and applies to every reader of this book, including the ones most confident it doesn't apply to them.

While reading about these mental processes won't make you immune to them, it can create a moment between hearing a claim and deciding what to think about it. A small gap between the feeling of certainty and treating that feeling as proof.

That gap is a small space between the evidence that exists and the conclusion the mind has already prepared. The space where propaganda operates. Where manufactured certainty takes hold, and where the difference between what's true and what merely feels true quietly disappears. In that pause there is room to ask a few simple questions.

Is this claim supported by evidence?

Have I heard it many times simply because it was repeated often?

What information might be missing?

Each chapter of this book takes one aspect that widens this gap and explores what it is, how it operates, what it feels like while it's running, and how far it reaches. A person who understands how that gap opens, and why, carries something practical into every charged conversation, every news cycle, and decision that matters.

It's a small space between stimulus and response. A brief moment between the feeling of certainty arriving and then settling in as fact. That gap, the brief pause before reacting, is where this book lives. It's the place where things can go differently.

Five Confessions.
No physical evidence.
Thirteen years in prison.

How can something like that happen?

CHAPTER 1

Smart People Fall for Lies Too

The Armor You Think You Have

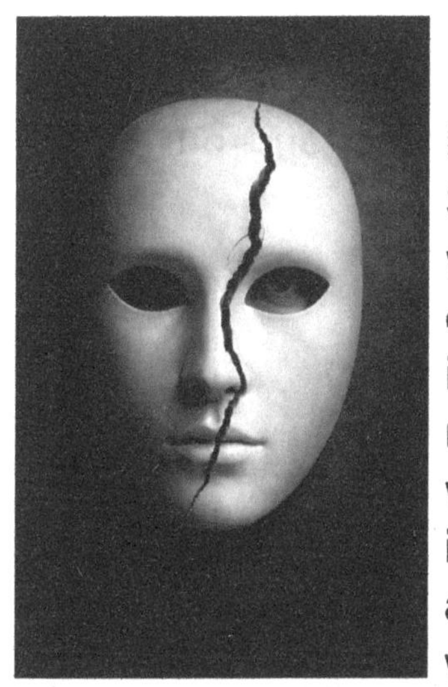

In 2003, the United States Secretary of State, sat before the United Nations Security Council and presented what he called "facts and conclusions based on solid intelligence.[1]" As a decorated, retired army general, he spoke with authority, using satellite imagery, audio recordings, and detailed diagrams. He wasn't a reckless man. He was considered one of the most credible figures in the American government.

The world watched.

Allies were persuaded.

The case for invading Iraq was built, in large part, on what he presented that day. Nearly everything he presented turned out to be wrong.

Colin Powell later called it the most painful moment of his career.[2] He wasn't stupid. He wasn't careless. He was a highly intelligent, experienced leader who'd been given selectively curated information that confirmed what the people around him already believed.[3]

His mind did the rest.

What happened to him on a global stage happens to all of us on a personal level, in our living rooms, our group chats, our workplaces, and our dinner tables, every single day.

The mental process is identical.

Only the stakes are different.

Everyone carries a silent, comforting belief that intelligence protects them from falling prey to believing something that isn't true. It lives just beneath the surface of how you see yourself and others. If you stay informed, you think you're surely safer and less likely to be fooled, misled, or emotionally manipulated.

The problem is that this belief, however reassuring, is entirely imagined.[4]

Intelligence helps you analyze arguments, understand complexity, and learn from experience. It's real, powerful, and valuable. However, your intelligence alone was never designed to protect you from manipulation.

The human mind didn't evolve to prioritize truth above all else. It evolved to prioritize safety and survival. It also evolved to prioritize social belonging, and emotional coherence. Long before you consciously evaluate whether something is true, your brain is already asking different questions.

Does this feel familiar?

Does this confirm what I already suspect?

Does this threaten my sense of safety or identity?

Those questions are automatic. They operate beneath awareness and influence what feels believable far more than you realize.

This is where the imagined protective barrier breaks down. Intelligence doesn't stand outside these processes calmly supervising them. It operates inside them and is shaped by them.[5]

When a claim aligns with your emotions, values, or social identity, your smart brain explains, justifies, and connects dots in ways that feel coherent and satisfying.

Now consider the reverse.

When a claim doesn't align with your emotions, values, or social identity, intelligence often steps in not as a neutral judge, but as a skilled defense attorney. Your brain again explains, justifies, and connects dots in ways that feel coherent and satisfying. At no point does this feel like manipulation; it feels like thinking.

The more intelligent you are, the more convincing your internal explanations become.[6] You can articulate your beliefs fluently, cite sources, construct narratives, and dismiss counterarguments with confidence. Those internal explanations can feel like clarity.

Understanding this is uncomfortable because it tells you that intelligence isn't a shield that places you above influence.

It's a tool.

This doesn't diminish intelligence.

It humanizes it.

Once you see that clearly, you're finally able to understand how smart, thoughtful, well-intentioned people fall for lies without ever realizing it.[7]

The Myth That Manipulation Only Happens to Other People

One of the most persistent and comforting myths about manipulation is the idea that it only works on other people, the ones who are not very smart or intelligent. You've heard it before, and maybe you've even thought to yourself, "I can't believe people are dumb enough to fall for that."

The thought feels satisfying because it draws a clean psychological boundary. There are the foolish people who get misled, and then there are people like you, rational and smart. However, this line is also imaginary.

Manipulation doesn't begin with stupidity; it begins with trust, then it targets attention, emotion, identity, and belonging. These aren't weaknesses unique to other people. They're universal human traits.[8]

Consider what happened to American physicians in the 1990s and early 2000s. These were some of the most educated professionals in the country, people who'd spent a decade in training and prided themselves on evidence based decision making.

Pharmaceutical representatives visited their offices with studies, charts, and confident clinical language. The message was consistent and repeated: a new class of opioid painkillers was far less addictive than previously thought.

Prescriptions climbed.

Patients became dependent.

Communities were devastated.

The doctors who prescribed these medications weren't naive or careless as a group. They were operating within a system that controlled the information they received, rewarded certainty over caution, and made the false narrative feel not only plausible but responsible.

When the full picture finally emerged, many doctors described a sense of profound disbelief, not because they'd been obviously deceived, but because the deception had been dressed in the language of science, authority, and care. Intelligence didn't protect them. The structure of the manipulation was built specifically to work on people who trusted data.

The deeper danger of the "stupid people" myth isn't just that it's inaccurate. The danger is that it blocks learning.[9] If your view is that manipulation only happens to stupid people, then reflection feels unnecessary, curiosity gets replaced by superiority, and conversations turn into ridicule, which rarely changes minds.

Letting go of this myth isn't about lowering your level of thinking. It's about raising awareness of how reasoning actually works. Once you stop asking "Who is dumb enough to believe this?" you can begin asking, "What psychological forces make this feel convincing?"

When Smart People Get It Wrong: Three Ordinary Stories

Jennifer P. is a middle school teacher. She is educated, thoughtful, politically moderate, someone who reads daily and considers herself skeptical. During a heated election season, widely circulated video shorts show a public figure making statements that seem outrageous.

They're repeated across multiple platforms, commentators reinforce the narrative, and her friends share them with concern.

She watches.

It feels shocking, and it also feels consistent with things she already suspects. She sends it to her sister before the third replay even finishes.

Later, full context emerges where the meaning of the video shifts dramatically when the entire speech is shown. By then, her emotional reaction had already formed. She'd discussed it at dinner, shared it in a group chat, and built a small narrative around it.

When the correction appears, it feels uncomfortable since the new information disrupts something she had already integrated into her worldview.[10]

She believed the original story because there was momentum from sharing and media manipulation, not because there was a failure of intelligence.

Now consider Steve S., a retired engineer who is analytical, detailed, and proud of his ability to evaluate data.

Steve listens to a podcast on his morning walk, coffee cooling in his hand, nodding along before he's even finished his first mile. The podcast frames financial news in a dramatic, almost apocalyptic way. The host uses charts, cites statistics, and speaks with total confidence.

The message repeats daily. At first he's skeptical, but repetition builds familiarity, and familiarity builds trust.

The predictions seem plausible, and gradually Steve begins making decisions built on the narrative. He shares warnings with friends and becomes emotionally invested.

Months later, many dramatic claims fail to materialize. The data was selectively interpreted, but by then the story feels personal.[11] It feels like insight he discovered, not messaging he absorbed.

This is what slow erosion looks like, not a single moment of deception, but a gradual rewriting of what feels true.

Now, let's examine Marcus's story.

Every few weeks, Marcus gets together with a close group of friends he's known for years. They are a smart, and curious bunch of people. It's the kind of group that argues about books and laughs loudly and genuinely cares about the world.

Over several months, a clear consensus forms among them about a particular health intervention. Nobody sits Marcus down and makes a case. Nobody sends him studies. The position simply saturates the atmosphere.

Skepticism, when it surfaces, gets met with a particular kind of silence, not hostile, just slightly uncomfortable, followed by a pivot to something else.

Agreement gets met with warmth, laughter, and the easy flow of people who are fully on the same page. Marcus finds himself nodding along, then repeating the group's conclusions at work, then defending them to his wife, who has different information.

It isn't until much later, when he reads something entirely outside his usual circle, that he realizes he never actually evaluated the claim himself. He adopted it because the social cost of not adopting it was quietly, consistently, too high. No dramatic deception occurred. The group had already decided, and social conformity did the rest.[12]

These three stories work through entirely different mechanisms. Jennifer was overwhelmed by repetition and emotional consistency. Steve was worn down gradually by a trusted, confident voice. Marcus never encountered false information at all. He was shaped by the invisible pressure of belonging.[13]

Manipulation rarely announces itself. It doesn't arrive with a villain's soundtrack. It arrives wrapped in something familiar: a trusted voice, a compelling statistic, a shared frustration, or simply the warmth of people who already agree. Being an expert can sometimes increase your vulnerability. When you're confident in your analytical skills, you may question things less often. You assume you'd notice manipulation. Because of that assumption, subtle influence slips through unnoticed.[14]

You might recognize yourself somewhere in these stories. Once you can see the pattern clearly in others, you can begin to see it honestly in yourself.

A new question emerges: if seeing the pattern clearly still isn't enough to protect you, what is? That's where we're going next.

Clarity Lives on the Other Side of Feeling Safe

If there's one thing that shuts down clear thinking faster than misinformation, it's shame. The moment you feel judged, mocked, or intellectually cornered, your brain shifts gears.

It stops listening, evaluating, and stops being curious. Your mind moves into protection mode which isn't interested in the truth. It's interested in survival. This is why emotional safety is the foundation for thinking clearly.

Think about a time when someone tried to correct you publicly. They didn't do it gently or privately. Maybe they were right and the facts were on their side, but what did your body do at that moment?

Your chest tightened, your heart rate shifted, and you felt the flush of shame creep over you. Your thoughts raced and you prepared a defense before you even finished hearing their point.

That reaction isn't stupidity; it's self-preservation.[15]

Shame runs deeper than a single uncomfortable moment. It shapes what you're willing to examine, and what you'll defend long past the point of reason. There's an entire chapter ahead devoted to understanding it fully, because it deserves that level of attention.

Now picture a conversation where no one is keeping score, a friend asks a genuine question rather than launching a correction. It's a moment where you feel curious rather than cornered. Notice how differently your mind opens up in that space.

Uncertainty feels interesting rather than threatening. You weren't suddenly smarter at that moment. You were simply safe enough to think.[16] That's what becomes possible when the temperature drops after things get heated.

Emotional safety doesn't mean avoiding hard topics. It means delivering and receiving meaningful conversations without triggering an identity meltdown. It means separating yourself from the belief. This kind of mature growth requires stability, not panic.

If your goal is to humiliate someone into clarity, you'll fail. If your goal is to create a space where questioning feels safe, you increase the odds of real dialogue, not instant agreement, but genuine thought.

Throughout this book, you'll return to this principle repeatedly. You can't think clearly when you feel under attack. You can't transform your own thoughts while judging yourself.

When your new goal is understanding, adopting gentle honesty with yourself is vital as you move through these pages.

What's ahead is a map of how the mind actually works under pressure, under repetition, and under the weight of belonging. By the end, you won't just understand why smart people fall for lies. You'll recognize the exact moment it happens, and you'll have the tools to pause when it does.

Chapter Summary

- Intelligence can help you reason, but it can also help you rationalize.
- Manipulation doesn't target low intelligence; it targets the universal human traits of emotion, identity, trust, and repetition.
- Labeling others as foolish prevents understanding. Labeling yourself as foolish prevents growth.

- Ordinary, thoughtful people are misled every day, not because they lack critical thinking, but because the narratives they encounter feel consistent, familiar, or emotionally compelling, and the social cost of disagreeing is sometimes simply too high.

- Shame shuts down reflection, and an attack triggers defensiveness. Calm curiosity creates space for clarity.

- To think more clearly, you must first create an environment, internally and externally, where questioning doesn't feel like humiliation.

CHAPTER 2

What Your Eyes See vs. What You Believe

The Witness Who Was Certain

In October 1992, a cargo plane crashed into two apartment buildings in Amsterdam, killing dozens of residents and the crew aboard.

It was a devastating and chaotic scene.

Researchers later began asking Dutch citizens whether they'd seen television footage of the moment the plane struck the building.[1]

The footage was vivid and specific in most descriptions.

No such footage existed. None had ever been broadcast, and no recording of the actual crash moment had ever been made.

When researchers followed up, a significant portion of respondents not only confirmed they'd seen the footage but added precise details. They recalled the speed, the trajectory, and the exact moment of impact.

They weren't lying. They weren't confused about whether they'd watched television coverage of the aftermath. They genuinely remembered seeing something that didn't exist.

Their minds had constructed the memory from fragments: news reports, photographs, prior knowledge of how plane crashes look, and the emotional weight of a tragedy that felt too large not to have been witnessed directly.

This isn't a story about their memory failing; it's a story about how the mind works. Your mind reconstructs your world constantly, using expectation, emotion, prior belief, and narrative as its building materials.

By the time something reaches your conscious awareness, it's already been shaped. What feels like direct observation is often far more constructed than you might imagine.

Your Brain Is Not a Camera

You trust your senses because they feel immediate. When you see something happen, the experience feels raw and direct, as though reality is entering your mind unfiltered. That feeling of immediacy is in itself a construction.[2]

Your brain isn't a passive recorder waiting for input. It's an active prediction machine. It constantly generates expectations about what it's about to perceive and then adjusts those expectations as new information comes in.[3]

Prior beliefs, emotional states, and existing narratives all influence which details get amplified and which get held back. Your expectations aren't separate from what you see. They're woven into perception before you're aware of seeing anything at all.

Think of it as a mental highlighter. Your beliefs decide what gets emphasized automatically, and everything else fades.

Emotion intensifies this further.

Anger emphasizes threat, fear amplifies danger, and pride expands validation.[4]

Once emotion enters the picture, interpretation begins to feel like certainty which creates the illusion that you're responding directly to reality rather than to your version of it.

That difference, between reality and your version of it, may sound subtle, but it isn't. It's the space that propaganda is designed to widen, and it's the pause that grows invisible the longer you go without noticing it.

The Conclusion That Arrives Before the Evidence

Psychologists have a name for what happens when your conclusions travel faster than your reasoning. It's called belief bias.[5]

When you encounter an argument, your mind doesn't evaluate the logic first; it evaluates the conclusion. If the conclusion agrees with what you already believe, the argument feels sound. You absorb it, share it, and easily move on.

If the conclusion disagrees with what you already believe, you scrutinize every source, question every method, and search for any flaw. It feels weak, even when the logical structure is identical in both cases.

Belief bias doesn't feel like bias; it feels like discernment. It feels like knowing what good reasoning looks like. That's precisely what makes it so durable. The filter is invisible because it feels like clarity.[6]

When the Evidence Loses

A city councilman that Diana A. has followed for years, is at the center of a local investigative piece. He is someone she's defended in conversations and quietly admired. The conclusion is unflattering. A pattern of redirecting public funds toward projects that benefited his personal network is uncovered.

Diana reads it and feels the friction before she reaches the second paragraph. Her mind moves fast. The journalist has an agenda. The sources are disgruntled former employees. The documents could be taken out of context. The timing is suspicious, with an election approaching. By the time she finishes reading, she hasn't evaluated the evidence. She's defended against it.

Now reverse the situation. Diana has always distrusted this councilman. She reads the same article, the same documents, and the same sources. Every detail confirms what she already knew. The neutral pause in one of his quoted responses reads as arrogance. A financial figure feels like proof of a pattern she long suspected. She doesn't scrutinize the methodology. She shares the article before finishing it.

Same evidence, two entirely different experiences of reading it. Diana isn't weak or irrational; she's doing exactly what human minds do when evidence collides with identity.[7]

Changing a belief isn't just an intellectual event; it carries social weight.[8] If Diana publicly praised this councilman, defended him in conversations, and built part of her civic identity around supporting him, then changing her mind means more than updating information. It means acknowledging she was wrong, visibly, to people who watched her be wrong.

The brain senses that exposure before the conscious mind articulates it. It registers the social risk and responds by protecting the belief, not because Diana is dishonest, but because belonging and coherence are among the most powerful forces the mind knows.

The Quiet Reward Your Brain Is Chasing

Something that doesn't get said often enough is that being right feels good. Not satisfying in an abstract sense, but neurologically good.

Research suggests that confirmation of existing beliefs activates reward-related regions, the same circuitry involved in other forms of positive reinforcement.[9]

When information agrees with what you already believe, your brain registers something close to pleasure: a small pulse of validation, a silent signal that you're competent, that your model of the world is accurate, and that you belong among people who see things correctly.

When information challenges your belief, the opposite happens. You experience friction, discomfort, and a faint but real sense of threat.

Your brain learns this pattern.

Agreement feels like safety.

A challenge feels like danger.

This isn't a conscious calculation. It happens before thinking begins. This is why debates rarely change minds and often harden them instead. The person across from you isn't just defending an idea. They're protecting a reward system.

When a belief is tied to values, moral commitments, or group membership, the cost rises sharply.[10] Changing your mind stops feeling like updating information and starts feeling like losing a piece of yourself.

The Story Running Before You Arrive

Beneath all of this, running constantly and quietly, is something even more fundamental than individual beliefs: the narrative structure that organizes them.[11]

Your mind isn't a collection of isolated opinions.

It's a storyteller.

Your mind is constructing a continuous account of what is happening, who is trustworthy, what is fair, what is dangerous, and what things mean. This narrative forms slowly, shaped by culture, experience, and repetition.

Once established, it doesn't wait for evidence.

It primes perception before evidence arrives.

Return to Diana. Her positive narrative about the councilman didn't form from a single impression. It accumulated across years of small confirmations: a speech she found compelling, a neighbor who vouched for him, and repeated exposure to his public presence. Each confirmation deepened the story.

By the time the investigative article appeared, the narrative wasn't a hypothesis she was testing. It was the lens through which she read the article.

If your story is that a particular group is dangerous, you ask what their latest transgression was. If your story is that they're misunderstood, you ask what context is being ignored.

The question filters reality before any fact enters the room. This is another reason why people consuming identical information reach opposite conclusions: the conclusions were partially written before the information arrived.

Both sides find evidence. Both feel real. Both believe the other side is selectively reading the situation. They're both right about the other, and they're both doing it themselves.[12]

What You Can Actually Do With This

Your own interpretations that have occasionally turned out to be wrong, weren't signs of poor reasoning. Your thoughts were finding meaning as fast as your brain was able to process them. That speed was at the expense of accuracy.

The same gaps that once helped you navigate uncertainty are the gaps that skilled manipulation finds first. Awareness doesn't close them entirely. It interrupts the automatic process long enough to matter.

When something feels instantly clear, instantly outrageous, or instantly validating, that feeling is worth pausing on. Not to distrust your senses entirely, but to ask one honest question.

Am I seeing this?

Am I interpreting this?

That pause doesn't need to be long. It doesn't require certainty or the abandonment of your existing views. It requires only a moment of curiosity about your own mind, a willingness to hold the question open a little longer before sealing it into a hard conclusion.

The gap between what your eyes see and what your mind decides it means is where manipulation lives. It's also, when you learn to notice it, where clarity begins. What you see is never just what is there. It's what you bring to it.

What comes next is the mechanism that makes that gap wider and harder to close: repetition. Understanding how it works will change the way you hear almost everything.[13]

Chapter Summary

- Your brain isn't a camera. It's a prediction machine that filters, fills, and shapes perception before conscious awareness begins.
- Belief bias means your mind judges conclusions before it evaluates reasoning. Agreeable conclusions feel logical, and uncomfortable ones feel flawed, even when the logic is identical.
- When evidence collides with identity, the mind almost always reframes the evidence rather than revising the belief. This isn't a weakness; it's the brain protecting coherence and belonging.

- Being right produces a neurological reward. Your brain learns to seek confirmation and avoid challenge, not through conscious choice but through pattern.

- Your mind runs a continuous narrative that decides what you notice before evidence arrives. Once that narrative becomes invisible, it feels like reality itself.

- The gap between perception and interpretation is where manipulation operates. Noticing that gap, even briefly, is where clearer thinking begins.

CHAPTER 3

The Illusory Truth Effect

The Claim That Became Common Knowledge

A statistic began circulating widely in America in the early 1990s. The claim was simple and striking: humans use only ten percent of their brains. It appeared in self help books, motivational speeches, classroom conversations, and eventually films.

By the time researchers began systematically surveying public belief, the majority of respondents accepted it as fact. Neuroscientists had never produced evidence supporting it. Decades of brain imaging research showed the opposite: virtually all brain regions are active and serve identifiable functions.

The claim wasn't just unverified.

It was demonstrably false.

The claim had been repeated so many times, across so many contexts, by so many different voices, that it had acquired the texture of established knowledge.[1]

That texture made the correction feel suspicious. When a neuroscientist appeared on television to debunk it, viewers often felt a faint skepticism toward the correction rather than toward the original claim.

The correction was new.

The claim was old.

The brain trusts what it has met before.

This is the illusory truth effect, and it's running in your mind right now, on dozens of claims you've never stopped to examine.

Familiarity Feels Like Fact

Your brain is solving a problem every moment of every day. The world delivers more information than any mind can fully evaluate. So, the brain developed a shortcut.

When a piece of information arrives that's been encountered before, the brain processes it more easily. That ease generates a quiet internal signal. It feels known. It feels settled and true. Psychologists call this processing fluency.[2]

Your brain doesn't consciously reason that it's heard something before and therefore it must be accurate. The logic never surfaces.

What surfaces is a feeling, a subtle sense of credibility that attaches itself to familiar claims without announcing its own origin. You don't feel the repetition working. You feel the conclusion it produced.

Think of it like a path through a forest. The first time you walk it, you have to pay attention and notice every turn. The tenth time, your feet find it without effort. The path feels right because it's worn.

The illusory truth effect works the same way. Repeated claims become worn paths. Walking them requires no effort, and effortlessness feels like correctness.

Slogans, repeated headlines, and short memorable phrases are so effective because they aren't designed to inform, they're designed to wear paths. The first time you encounter a claim, you may question it. The fifth time, it feels less controversial. The tenth time, it feels almost obvious. Nothing about the evidence changed, only the familiarity did.

Repetition works even when people have been explicitly told a statement is false, and that's what makes this finding genuinely unsettling.[3] The brain remembers the statement more readily than it remembers the correction.

The warning fades.

The familiarity remains.

Correction is fighting on unfamiliar ground. The false claim has the advantage of the worn path.

Familiarity and accuracy feel identical, but they're entirely different things. A world saturated with repeated headlines and recycled claims produces far more passive exposure than active evaluation. The feeling of "I've heard this before" is not the same as "I've examined this carefully." That distinction carries enormous weight.

The Person Who Never Decided to Believe It

Rachel N. considers herself resistant to manipulation. Over about eighteen months, she keeps encountering a particular claim about a common food additive. It appears first in a health newsletter she receives, then in a podcast she listens to while commuting, then a friend mentions it at dinner.

A short video surfaces in her social media feed, citing a study she doesn't read. Another friend asks whether she's heard about it. A wellness blog she follows references it in passing as something readers probably already know.[4]

Rachel never sits down and decides to believe the claim. She never evaluates the evidence in any formal sense. She doesn't need to. The sixth or seventh encounter is enough. The claim no longer feels like something she's still considering. It feels like something she knows. She mentions it to her brother. She also factors it into her grocery shopping.

A registered dietitian publishes a piece explaining why the original claim misrepresents the research. Rachel reads the first two paragraphs and feels a familiar friction. Something about the correction feels off, not because she's examined it and found it wanting, but because it contradicts something that has already settled into her thoughts as an established fact.

The correction is accurate. Rachel's response isn't a failure of intelligence, it's a demonstration of exactly how the illusory truth effect operates in an ordinary mind. She didn't choose to believe the claim. The claim simply became familiar enough that belief followed without being invited.

Your thoughts don't require low intelligence or a weak character to fall victim to the illusory truth effect. They only require repetition and time.

How the Information Environment Makes This Worse

Rachel's experience didn't happen in a vacuum. It happened inside a specific kind of information environment, one built by the logic of its own incentives to repeat things.

Modern information moves fast.

Headlines are short.

Videos are brief.

Quotes are extracted from context.

The same claim appears across platforms in slightly different forms, It is summarized, reposted, debated, and rephrased. Each encounter deepens familiarity. The system doesn't need to coordinate. It just needs to move.

Headlines carry particular weight because most people encounter them without reading what follows. A headline becomes a mental anchor.

The headline becomes the lasting impression, even when the article beneath it tells a more complicated story. Short statements travel further than careful explanations.[5] A ten-second video circulates thousands of times while a forty-minute documentary remains largely unwatched.

The brain doesn't reward how long something is.

It rewards quick recognition.

None of it requires a conspiracy. It requires incentives. Attention is the currency, and content that provokes a strong emotional response that gets shared.[6]

Shared content gets repeated. Repeated content builds familiarity. Familiarity builds perceived truth.

What feels established may simply be what was repeated most. Frequency isn't the truth. Repetition isn't validation. A fast moving information environment makes them feel identical, but they are not.

Why Ordinary People Spread What Isn't True

Most misinformation doesn't begin with bad intentions. That's one of the most important points in this chapter. Most people imagine misinformation as deliberate deception: someone crafting a false claim and releasing it knowing it's untrue.

Sometimes that happens.

A far larger portion of misinformation travels through a different mechanism entirely. Ordinary people share things that feel true, because those things are familiar, because they're emotionally resonant, and because sharing them feels responsible.[7]

Return to Rachel. She forwarded the food additive article to her brother without verifying it first. She didn't need to. Everything she'd already encountered made it feel verified. Sharing felt like protecting someone she cared about.

This is the human engine beneath spreading misinformation. People share because a claim aligns with something they already believe. They share because it feels urgent. They share because others they respect are sharing it.

Social endorsement adds weight to a claim regardless of whether the claim is accurate.[8] Widespread acceptance makes a claim feel safer to accept. Skepticism, when people you trust are passing something along, can feel almost antisocial.

Very few people think "I am spreading misinformation." They think "People should know this." That distinction matters enormously.

Misinformation ecosystems aren't sustained primarily by deception. They're sustained by ordinary human psychology moving at the speed of a share button.[9]

Familiarity, emotion, social validation, and speed together don't require coordinated malice for false narratives to travel far. Responding, connecting, and repeating, the things humans do naturally, is enough to carry them.

Understanding this shifts the entire frame. Instead of asking "Who is lying?" the more useful question becomes "What conditions make this easy to spread?"

Misinformation travels through ordinary psychological processes, which means understanding those processes is the most powerful tool available, not to eliminate error entirely, but to interrupt it.

What You Can Do With This

You won't stop encountering repetition. The information environment won't slow down. Rachel's experience isn't unusual; it's the default. What changes is whether you notice the mechanism while it's running.

One question does a surprising amount of work: have I heard this before, or do I actually know this?

Hearing something repeatedly is passive. Knowing something means you've examined it, traced it to a source, and tested it against alternative explanations. Most of what feels like knowledge is closer to accumulated familiarity. It's simply how your mind handles complexity, not a flaw in your character.

The vulnerability arrives the moment you stop distinguishing between the two.

Interrogating everything would be paralyzing, and that's not what is required. When a claim feels obvious, settled, or beyond question, that feeling is worth examining. Obvious and settled are often just other words for frequently repeated words. The claim that feels most certain deserves at least one honest question: where did this certainty come from?

What comes next examines the forces that make certain beliefs feel not just familiar but personally essential: the point where belief stops being an opinion and starts feeling like identity. That shift changes everything about how we hold ideas and how hard we fight to keep them.[10]

Chapter Summary

- The illusory truth effect means repetition alone increases perceived truth. The brain mistakes ease of recognition for evidence of accuracy.

- Familiarity and accuracy feel identical, but they're entirely different things. One comes from exposure; the other requires examination.

- The information environment is structured to repeat. Headlines, short videos, and shared content build familiarity at scale without requiring coordination or intent.

- Most misinformation spreads through ordinary human psychology, not deliberate deception. People share what feels true, urgent, and socially validated.

- The most useful interruption is a single honest question: have I heard this, or do I actually know this? That distinction, applied at the right moment, is where clearer thinking begins.

CHAPTER 4

Shame, Identity, and Defensiveness

The Moment Everything Became Personal

In 1982, a young researcher named Barry Marshall became convinced that stomach ulcers were caused by a bacterial infection.[1] The prevailing medical consensus held that ulcers resulted from stress and excess stomach acid. Marshall had evidence: cultures, observations, and a hypothesis that matched the data.

He presented his findings to the medical community and was largely dismissed. Gastroenterologists with decades of authority in the field didn't simply disagree with him. They ridiculed him. His work was rejected by major journals. Audiences were skeptical to the point of contempt when he presented his findings at various scientific conferences.

The medical establishment didn't double down because the evidence was weak. Marshall's evidence was strong enough that he eventually drank a petri dish of the bacteria himself to prove the point, developed gastritis, treated it with antibiotics, and recovered. He won the Nobel Prize in 2005.[2]

The establishment doubled down because the evidence threatened something larger than a theory. It threatened careers built on the old model, reputations staked on its authority, and identities constructed around being the experts who understood ulcers.

Accepting Marshall meant accepting that decades of confident medical practice had caused unnecessary suffering. That is not an intellectual update. That is a collapse of self.

Guilt Says You Did Something Shame Says You Are Something

Psychologists draw a sharp distinction between guilt and shame, and that distinction changes everything about how belief revision works.[3]

Guilt is specific. It attaches to an action: "I got that wrong." Guilt is uncomfortable, but manageable, because it leaves the self intact. You made an error and you can correct it. The person you are remains functional.

Shame is global. It attaches to identity: "I am someone who gets things wrong." Shame doesn't target the mistake. It targets the person who made it. That difference is enormous because it means correcting a belief doesn't just feel like updating information. It feels like confirming something damaging about who you are.

When a belief is challenged, the brain runs a rapid assessment. If the belief is lightly held and not connected to identity, the assessment is quick and relatively painless, new information arrives, and an adjustment is made. The process is complete.

When the belief is deeply held, publicly expressed, or tied to a group you belong to, everything shifts.[4] The question stops being "Is this true?" and becomes "What does being wrong about this say about me?"

That second question is where shame lives. Once activated, shame isn't interested in accuracy. It's interested in survival.

The Person Who Couldn't Afford to Change Her Mind

Consider Nadia S., a high school history teacher who spent three years publicly and passionately advocating a particular interpretation of a controversial local historical event. She wrote about it in the school newsletter. She taught it in her classroom. She defended it at a community meeting when a parent challenged her.

She organized a small reading group around it. The interpretation had become the lens through which she understood her town's identity, and by extension, her own role within it.

A historian later published new archival research. The documents were detailed and credibly sourced. The evidence didn't just complicate Nadia's interpretation. It substantially undermined it.

Nadia read the research carefully. She understood it. Privately, somewhere she didn't fully articulate even to herself, she recognized its weight. Publicly she said nothing.

She didn't update her curriculum. She didn't mention the new findings to her reading group. When a colleague brought it up in the staff room, she said the historian had a particular agenda and that primary sources were always subject to interpretation.

She wasn't lying, exactly. She was doing something more human than lying. She was protecting a version of herself that had become real through three years of public commitment. Changing her mind meant dismantling her public identity. The intellectual cost of revision was low. The social and psychological cost felt catastrophic.[5]

This isn't a story about a dishonest teacher. It's a story about what happens when a belief stops being something you hold and starts being something you are.

When Belonging Makes Beliefs Load Bearing

You've already seen how social belonging shapes how you think. Marcus stayed inside a group's consensus not through deception but through the powerful pull of wanting to remain one of them. Nadia's situation shows that same mechanism operating at higher emotional stakes. The element at risk wasn't just social comfort, it was professional identity.[6]

Beliefs rarely exist in isolation. They exist inside groups. Shared beliefs communicate loyalty, values, and alignment. When a belief becomes central to a group you belong to, holding it confirms who you are in relation to other people. It signals belonging.

This is why certain debates feel disproportionately intense. Two people can discuss the same evidence calmly when neither person's group membership is implicated. The moment evidence touches a belief that is crucial for identity and belonging, the conversation changes.

The more central a belief is to a group's identity, the more dangerous revision becomes socially. Changing your mind can feel like stepping away from the people who matter to you. It can feel like signaling you were never really one of them.

Nadia's reading group wasn't pressuring her directly. Nobody issued a threat. Revision would have required not just intellectual honesty but a kind of social courage that most people, understandably, find difficult when the stakes feel personal.

The more flexible an identity, the more flexible a belief.

Someone whose sense of self is built around curiosity and willingness to revise their thoughts finds that changing their mind strengthens rather than threatens who they are.[7]

Someone whose identity is built around certainty and group loyalty finds that changing your mind feels like betrayal.

Why Correction Hardens What It Tries to Soften

As you learned earlier, when someone presents evidence that challenges a belief you hold, your mind begins moving away from the evidence. You're already searching for the flaw, or the missing context. Your defense was activated before the argument was complete.

Psychologists call this motivated reasoning.[8] The brain doesn't experience it as defensiveness. It experiences it as critical thinking. The scrutiny feels legitimate.

From the inside, you're simply being careful. From the outside, you're protecting a belief from evidence.[9]

Public challenge intensifies this dramatically. Accepting a correction publicly can feel like losing status, appearing inconsistent, or admitting that people who trusted your judgment were wrong to do so. The mind works very hard to avoid that outcome.

Return to Nadia. When her colleague raised the historian's findings in the staff room, Nadia had an audience. The response she gave, questioning the historian's agenda, wasn't generated by careful analysis of the historian's methodology. It was generated by the presence of other people watching her respond to a challenge.

The audience transformed a question about evidence into a question about her standing. It was about who she was in that room, in that school, and in that community. It was now a question of whether the correction would diminish her in the eyes of the people whose respect she had earned.

Public shaming makes this worse, not better. When people are mocked or humiliated for a belief, the belief almost always becomes more entrenched.[10] The conversation shifts from accuracy to dignity. The person is no longer asking whether they are right. They are asking whether they are safe.

Safety and accuracy rarely coexist when shame is present.

Facts delivered as weapons produce defensive armor, not openness. The person across from you isn't refusing to think. They're thinking very hard about how to protect themselves from you.

What You Can Do With This

This pattern has run through Marshall, through Nadia, through the staff room, and through the quiet social rules of every group that uses belief as a signal of belonging. It runs through you too. Recognizing that, without immediately turning it into a reason for self judgment, is where the work begins.

The next time you feel a strong urge to defend a personal belief being challenged, pause before responding, not to suppress the defense, but to ask one honest question. Are you protecting the truth, or are you protecting your image?

The same question applies when you're on the other side, when you're the one offering a correction. Delivering evidence as an attack produces defensive armor. Delivering it as a genuine question preserves dignity and keeps the other person's mind open.[11]

"I came across something that complicated my thinking on this. What do you make of it?" isn't a weak approach. It's the approach most likely to produce actual reconsideration.

The Armor That Costs More Than It Protects

Every time you defend a belief against credible evidence purely to protect your image, the belief becomes harder and harder to question. Your emotional investment increases. Eventually, it isolates you from the honest internal examination that makes growth possible.

Nadia's reading group met for another year after the archival research was published. She never mentioned it. The history she taught remained unchanged.

Nadia lost the opportunity to model something rare and genuinely valuable for her students. It was the kind of intellectual honesty that says, "I learned something new, and it changed what I thought I knew." That moment, had she allowed it, would have taught more than any curriculum.

Changing your mind isn't a weakness. It's evidence that your thinking is alive. The ability to change your mind is the most powerful critical thinking tool available, and you can't reason your way into that capacity. You have to feel safe enough to try.[12]

What comes next examines how the people and environments around you shape the social landscape of belief that determines, often invisibly, which ideas feel possible and which feel forbidden.[13]

Chapter Summary

- Shame transforms intellectual correction into an identity threat. Guilt says you made a mistake. Shame says you are the mistake. That difference determines whether revision feels possible or intolerable.

- Beliefs become load bearing when tied to group membership, public commitment, or personal narrative. Challenging them stops feeling like a question about evidence and starts feeling like a question about belonging.

- Defensiveness is protection, not stubbornness. When correction arrives as an attack, the mind stops evaluating evidence and starts managing the threat. Public shame hardens beliefs rather than loosening them.

- The honest question under challenge isn't "Am I right?" It's "Am I protecting the truth, or am I protecting my image?" Those two motivations produce entirely different responses.

- Minds change when the emotional cost of being wrong drops low enough for curiosity to rise. Safety is the primary condition for growth.

CHAPTER 5

The Blind Spot in the Expert's Eye

The Doctor Who Couldn't See What Was There

Women giving birth in European hospitals died at alarming rates from a condition called childbed fever throughout most of the nineteenth century. The mortality rate in some wards reached thirty percent. Mothers who delivered at home, attended by midwives with no formal medical training, survived at far higher rates. The pattern was visible in the data for decades.

Ignaz Semmelweis, a Hungarian physician working in Vienna in the 1840s, noticed the pattern and traced it to a source.[1] Doctors and medical students were moving directly from performing autopsies to delivering babies without washing their hands. Midwives did not perform autopsies.

Semmelweis introduced mandatory handwashing with a chlorinated solution in his ward. Mortality dropped from roughly ten percent to under two percent almost immediately.

The medical establishment rejected his findings, not because the data was unclear; the data was solid. They rejected it because accepting it meant accepting that physicians, the educated professionals, the trained experts, the people whose hands were supposed to heal, had been killing the patients in their care.

The conclusion wasn't just scientifically uncomfortable. It was professionally catastrophic. It threatened the identity physicians had built their professional lives around.

Semmelweis died in an asylum in 1865. He never knew that years later Germ theory would vindicate him entirely.

The doctors who rejected Semmelweis weren't stupid. They were operating inside a blind spot so thoroughly integrated into their professional identity that the evidence couldn't reach them. They weren't refusing to see. They genuinely couldn't. That is what a real blind spot does. It doesn't feel like avoidance. It feels like clear thinking.

The Gap You Can't See From Where You Stand

A blind spot isn't a lack of information. It's a gap in awareness, a place where your thinking feels complete while being incomplete. The most dangerous situation is the one you never think to question.

Consider how this works in a car. When you know your mirrors have blind spots, you compensate. You check carefully before changing lanes. You build the limitation into your behavior. Now imagine believing your mirrors show everything. You'd check less often, not because you're careless, but because you're certain you won't hit someone else.

Intellectual confidence works the same way. Smart people trust their analytical skills, and most of the time that trust is earned. When belief, emotion, or identity subtly shape perception, intelligence doesn't necessarily catch it.[2] It may simply help justify it.

The reasoning feels sound. The conclusion feels earned. The blind spot stays invisible because nothing from inside it signals that something is missing.

Most people agree that cognitive biases affect human judgment. The same people, when asked whether those biases affect their own judgment, consistently rate themselves as less biased than average. Psychologists call this pattern the bias blind spot.[3]

Knowledge about bias doesn't eliminate bias. It relocates it. Blind spots are especially persistent when socially reinforced.

When everyone around you shares your perspective, the blind spot never gets exposed. Agreement feels like validation and accuracy. The problem is the assumption that you are already seeing things clearly.

The Person Who Knew About Bias and Had It Anyway

Thomas R. is a journalist who has written about cognitive bias and interviewed the researchers who study it. His professional familiarity with the subject is precisely what makes him uniquely unaware of his own blind spot.

Over several years, Thomas developed a strong interpretive framework for understanding a particular economic policy debate. His framework was informed, carefully constructed, and widely respected among colleagues who shared his general orientation. He built a body of published work around it. Without him fully realizing it, that became part of how he understood his own credibility.

A research paper was published that challenged a core assumption in his framework. The methodology was sound. The data was extensive. The conclusions were carefully qualified.

Thomas read it. He noticed, somewhere in the first few pages, a faint resistance. He continued reading and the resistance grew. He found himself scrutinizing the methodology more intensely than he would for a paper confirming his view. He noted limitations. He questioned the framing. He drafted a response in his head before finishing the paper.

He never decided to dismiss it. He simply engaged with it far more critically than its quality warranted, and far less openly than he would have engaged with supporting evidence. By the time he finished reading, the paper felt weaker to him than it actually was.[4]

Thomas knew about motivated reasoning. He had written about it. That knowledge did nothing to interrupt the process as it ran. The sophistication of his understanding became, in that moment, an additional layer of cover. He wasn't dismissing the paper. He was carefully evaluating it.

It felt like rigor.

It was protection.

This is the bias blind spot operating in a mind that knows exactly what the bias blind spot is.

What Emotion Lights Up and What It Leaves Dark

Emotion acts like a spotlight. It doesn't change what's in the room. It changes what gets illuminated. The more emotionally invested you are in a belief, the more efficiently your attention finds evidence supporting it.

Details that align with your position stand out immediately. They feel important and relevant. Details that complicate or contradict your position tend to recede, not because you decide to ignore them, but because the spotlight isn't pointing there.[5]

This is what Thomas experienced without naming it. When he read the challenging paper, his attention sharpened toward its weaknesses. When he reads confirming research, his attention moves more smoothly across the whole.

The same analytical capacity, directed by different emotional stakes, produces different levels of scrutiny. Neither feels biased. Both feel like careful reading.

Over time, selective attention creates a distorted sense of the evidence landscape. What feels like overwhelming support may simply reflect where the spotlight has consistently pointed. The territory feels mapped because you've walked it so many times.

The parts you haven't walked, the evidence you've attended to least carefully, remain unmapped. Unmapped territory doesn't announce itself. It just stays dark.

Reducing emotional investment isn't always possible or even desirable. Caring about ideas is part of thinking seriously about them. The more useful practice is noticing when emotion is doing the work of evaluation. Ask yourself:

If I cared less about being right on this, what might I be reading differently?

The Architecture That Influences Your Thoughts

You've already seen how identity makes certain beliefs feel personally essential, how the whole self can feel at stake when a belief is challenged. When that dynamic operates not just inside one mind but across an entire environment, something more powerful and less visible takes hold.

Every community, professional culture, political tribe, or social group builds what might be called a belief architecture. It is an invisible structure that determines which ideas feel reasonable, which feel radical, and which feel so obviously wrong they barely register as worth considering.

This architecture isn't maintained through explicit rules. It's maintained through tone, through what gets praised and what gets ignored, through which questions are treated as serious and which are met with a look that says you should already know the answer to that.[6]

Thomas's professional community has this architecture. Certain analytical frameworks carry status. Certain conclusions signal sophistication.

Certain questions, if raised publicly, would mark the questioner as someone who doesn't quite understand how things work.

Thomas doesn't experience this as pressure. He experiences it as shared understanding. The architecture is invisible precisely because it has been so thoroughly internalized.[7]

This is how intelligent communities arrive at entirely different interpretations of the same reality, not because one side lacks the capacity to reason clearly, but because each community's architecture has shaped what counts as reasonable, what counts as evidence, and which conclusions feel like common sense versus which feel like they require extraordinary justification.

The more thoroughly you've absorbed a community's architecture, the less visible it becomes. It stops feeling like a framework and starts feeling like the world. A framework that feels like the world is the most effective blind spot of all, because nothing inside it generates the signal that says look more carefully here.

The Distance Between Knowing and Seeing

There's a version of reading this book that feels intellectually satisfying without changing anything. You understand the mechanisms. You recognize the patterns. You can describe confirmation bias, motivated reasoning, and the illusory truth effect with genuine accuracy. You leave each chapter feeling more informed without feeling more accountable.

That gap, between knowing and seeing, is where this chapter lives.

Awareness is knowing that cognitive biases exist. Insight is catching one operating in your own thinking in real time. Those are entirely different experiences, and the distance between them is larger than most people expect.[8]

Awareness is also fast. Reading about bias happens at the speed of comprehension. Insight is slow. It requires noticing a reaction before acting on it, questioning a conclusion before defending it, and sitting with discomfort long enough to ask whether the discomfort is a signal or background noise. That slowness runs directly against the grain of environments that reward speed, certainty, and confident conclusions.

Thomas felt this. His familiarity with motivated reasoning didn't interrupt it. It gave him more sophisticated language for the justification it produced. Knowing the name of the pattern didn't slow the pattern down.

Objectivity is not a switch. It is a discipline. It requires building habits that deliberately introduce friction into confident conclusions, not as self-punishment, not as a performance of humility, but as a genuine practice of intellectual honesty.[9]

The goal isn't eliminating bias. The goal is shortening the distance between reaction and reflection. It's about noticing sooner, questioning faster, and pausing before conclusions harden into certainty.

Awareness gives you the vocabulary. Insight changes what you actually do. What you do, not what you know, is what determines whether your thinking actually gets clearer.

What You Can Do With This

Two practical questions introduced in this chapter are worth sitting alongside each other. The first is this:

If I cared less about being right on this, what might I be reading differently?

The second is equally pointed.

If this claim came from outside my community, would I evaluate it the same way?

Neither question is comfortable. That discomfort is the point. A question that produces no friction is a question your blind spot has already absorbed.

The questions that make you pause, that make you want to immediately qualify or explain why they don't quite apply here, those are the ones worth examining.

Thomas's blind spot wasn't visible from inside his framework. It became partially visible the moment he noticed his own resistance and asked what was generating it, not as an accusation, but as genuine curiosity.

Noticing it didn't eliminate the pattern. It created a small gap between the automatic response and the conclusion the automatic response was producing. That gap is where clearer thinking becomes possible.

You won't see all your blind spots. That's the nature of them. The question isn't whether you have blind spots. You do, and everyone does. The question is whether you've made it safe enough, internally, to look for them without feeling like looking is an attack on who you are.

What comes next examines the difference between manipulation as an accidental byproduct of human psychology and manipulation as a deliberate strategy, deployed by people who understand exactly what they're doing and why it works.[10]

Chapter Summary

- The bias blind spot means knowledge about bias doesn't eliminate bias. People who understand cognitive bias consistently rate themselves as less affected by it than others. Awareness of the problem doesn't become evidence of immunity from it.

- Emotion acts as a spotlight. It doesn't change what's available but changes what gets illuminated.

- Emotional investment makes confirming details vivid and complicating details dim, without the filtering feeling like filtering.

- Every community builds a belief architecture that shapes which ideas feel reasonable, which feel radical, and which feel unworthy of serious consideration. The more thoroughly it's internalized, the less visible it becomes.

- The distance between awareness and insight is larger than expected. Knowing that biases exist is fast and satisfying. Catching one operating in your own thinking in real time requires slowness, friction, and a tolerance for discomfort that confident environments rarely reward.

- Objectivity is not a switch. It is a discipline. The goal isn't eliminating bias. It's shortening the gap between reaction and reflection: noticing sooner, questioning faster, and pausing before conclusions harden into certainty.

CHAPTER 6

When Manipulation Becomes a Strategy

The Campaign That Knew What It Was Doing

A research firm called Cambridge Analytica claimed it had developed a method for large scale psychological targeting of voters in the years leading up to the 2016 United States presidential election.[1] The firm harvested data from tens of millions of Facebook profiles without explicit consent. It built detailed psychological profiles of individual voters, and used those profiles to serve precisely tailored political messaging.

Fearful personalities received messages emphasizing threat. Identity conscious voters received messages built around belonging and pride. Grievance oriented profiles received content designed to deepen existing resentments.

The firm's internal communications, later made public through whistleblower testimony and parliamentary investigations, revealed something important. The people designing these campaigns were not simply running advertisements. They were applying documented psychological research to the deliberate engineering of belief.

They understood confirmation bias. They understood emotional priming. They understood that identity targeted messaging bypasses analytical evaluation because it doesn't ask you to think. It asks you to recognize yourself. Whether these methods were as effective as the firm claimed remains disputed, but the intent and the approach are documented.[2]

This was not manipulation as an accidental byproduct of human psychology. This was manipulation as a studied, deliberate strategy, designed by people who had read the same research this book draws on, and who chose to use it as a toolkit. That distinction is what this chapter is about.

The Difference That Changes Everything

Everything examined so far in this book has described manipulation as something that emerges from the ordinary operation of human minds. Repetition creates false familiarity. Identity protects belief from evidence.

Blind spots hide inside expertise. Social architecture shapes what feels like clear thinking. None of this requires a villain. It requires only humans being human in environments that happen to exploit those tendencies.

This chapter introduces a different category. Some manipulation is deliberate. Someone on the other side of the message understands the mechanisms described in this book, understands your psychological architecture, and is using that understanding to engineer a specific response in you, while ensuring you experience that response as your own free conclusion.

The difference between accidental and deliberate manipulation is not about the experience of being manipulated. Both feel identical from the inside. Both feel like thinking. The difference is entirely on the other side of the message, in whether someone designed it to work on you specifically.

The Person Who Was Targeted

Elena B. is a middle aged nurse who spent seven months in an online community organized around health and wellness. She joined after a difficult personal experience with the medical system: a misdiagnosis that cost her months of unnecessary treatment.

She was skeptical of institutional medicine in a way that felt earned and specific to her experience.

The community felt warm and knowledgeable.

Members shared research, personal stories, and a sense of being people who had done their homework rather than simply accepting what they were told.

Elena valued that framing. It matched her own concept of who she is, someone who questions, investigates, and thinks independently.

What she didn't know, and what took her more than a year to piece together, was that the community's most active voices were coordinated.[3] Several of the accounts she trusted most had been created specifically to cultivate exactly the profile she represented.

They targeted people who were medically skeptical, self identified as independent thinkers, emotionally primed by personal grievance, and socially isolated from mainstream medical networks. The content those accounts shared was not random. It followed a documented escalation pattern, beginning with claims that were largely accurate, building trust through credibility, then gradually introducing more extreme positions as the community's shared identity deepened.

Elena didn't feel manipulated during those seven months. She felt informed. She felt like she was finally seeing clearly, accessing information that mainstream sources were ignoring or suppressing.

The community's framing gave her not just beliefs but an identity as someone who sees through inaccurate claims. That identity became the most powerful part of the manipulation.[4] Once the identity was in place, challenging the beliefs felt like challenging who she was.

The moment she discovered the coordination behind the community's most trusted voices, her first response wasn't clarity.

It was grief.

Something she had experienced as genuine connection and genuine insight had been engineered. She hadn't been reasoning her way to conclusions. She had been guided there by people who understood exactly how her mind would move.

Psychologists researching what they call the Dark Triad, a cluster of traits combining Machiavellianism, narcissism, and psychopathy, have identified a personality profile that's significantly more comfortable treating other people as instruments rather than as individuals.[5]

Those high in these traits aren't confused about what they're doing. They understand social and psychological dynamics clearly, and they apply that understanding without the discomfort that would slow most people down. They intentionally manipulate others for their own gain.

The accounts coordinating Elena's community weren't operating from blind spots. They were operating from a deliberate choice to exploit hers. That doesn't make her naive for being susceptible. She was specifically targeted.

How Deliberate Manipulation Uses What You've Already Learned

The mechanisms in Elena's story are familiar because this book has already examined them. What's different is their source.

Repetition created familiarity. The same claims appeared across multiple trusted voices until they felt settled and obvious. This is the illusory truth effect, described earlier, deployed intentionally rather than accidentally.[6]

Identity was the primary target. The community didn't just present claims. It offered Elena a self concept as someone who thinks independently, someone who sees through institutional deception, and someone whose personal experience of being failed by the system was not an isolated incident but evidence of a pattern. Once that identity was established, the claims attached to it became personally essential rather than merely informational.[7]

Emotional priming was presented before every significant belief shift. Elena noticed, looking back, that the content she encountered always made her feel something before it asked her to believe something.

Fear about suppressed treatments.

Outrage about institutional negligence.

The warm validation of being told she was someone who saw what others missed. That emotional state was already in place before the claim arrived, creating the conditions in which the claim felt not just plausible but obvious.[8]

Social proof was manufactured. The apparent consensus within the community, the sense that many thoughtful, informed people had arrived at the same conclusions, was not organic. It was produced by coordinated accounts creating the appearance of independent agreement. The brain reads apparent consensus as evidence. Manufactured consensus exploits that reading deliberately.[9]

Memory and experience were reframed. Elena's actual medical experience, real and legitimately frustrating, was gradually reinterpreted through the community's narrative until it became not just her story but confirmation of a larger truth the community had already decided.

Personal experience is the most convincing evidence a mind can encounter.[10] Manipulators who understand this don't contradict your experience. They reinterpret it.

The sophistication of this approach is not incidental. It reflects deliberate knowledge of psychological research, applied with the specific goal of bypassing the defenses this book is trying to build.

What Propaganda Does That Ordinary Influence Doesn't

Propaganda is large scale manipulation. The same psychological mechanisms operate here, but the reach, the resources, and the intentionality behind them are amplified to the point where entire populations can be influenced without any individual feeling persuaded.[11]

The most effective propaganda doesn't announce itself as propaganda. It presents itself as common sense, as what everyone already knows, as the obvious conclusion that only confused or compromised people would resist. It doesn't ask you to believe something new. It asks you to recognize something you've always suspected was true.

This framing, "people like you already know this," is among the most powerful tools available to deliberate manipulators because it combines identity targeting with social proof and bypasses the brain's evaluation of the claim entirely.[12] You're not being asked to assess evidence. You're being invited to confirm your own intelligence and group membership simultaneously. The conclusion arrives not as a proposition to be examined but as a recognition to be felt.

The goal of propaganda is to make you feel that your mind was never changed, that you simply finally understood something that was always true. That subjective experience of clarity, of finally seeing, is the manipulation's most complete achievement. It's also the most durable product of that achievement, because a conclusion that feels like you created it's far more resistant to revision than one that was obviously received.[13]

What You Can Do With This

Recognizing deliberate manipulation is harder than recognizing accidental manipulation because it's designed to be invisible. There are patterns to look for in seeing deliberate deception.

The first is identity before evidence. When a message leads with who you are rather than what it's claiming, when it establishes your membership in a group of clear sighted people before presenting any information, the identity framing is doing preparatory work. It's building the context in which the claim will be received before you've evaluated the claim. Notice that sequence.

The second is emotional activation before content. Genuine information can produce emotional responses. Deliberate manipulation typically reverses the order. The emotional state, fear, outrage, urgency, or the warm validation of being told you see what others miss, arrives before the substantive claim. When you notice strong emotion without yet having encountered a clear, examinable argument, that sequence is worth pausing on.

The third is manufactured consensus. Ask how you know that many people believe something. If the evidence of consensus comes from within the same community presenting the claim, the consensus and the claim share the same source. That's not independent confirmation. That's circular reinforcement.

The fourth is the escalation pattern. Deliberate manipulation campaigns rarely begin with their most extreme claims. They begin with credible information, build trust and identity, then move gradually toward positions you would have rejected at the outset.

When you notice that your current views on a topic are significantly more extreme than your views six months ago, and the movement happened inside a single community or information source, the escalation pattern is worth examining.

The most clarifying question you can ask yourself is whether you're arriving at these conclusions independently, or whether you're being guided to them.

The Point Where Knowledge Becomes Protection

Elena's story doesn't end in the community. It ends two years later, when she works as a volunteer with a health literacy organization that helps people evaluate medical information. She describes the experience of being deliberately targeted not with bitterness but with a kind of precise clarity.

She says she's more careful now not because she trusts less but because she understands more: about how her mind moves, about what identity targeted messaging feels like from the inside, and about the difference between the feeling of clarity and the evidence of it.

The knowledge this book builds is not a guarantee. Deliberate manipulators are skilled and motivated and they will continue to develop new approaches. Knowledge changes the texture of the experience, though.

When you understand that the feeling of finally seeing clearly can itself be engineered, you hold that feeling a little more carefully before letting it harden into certainty.

Being deliberately targeted doesn't make you stupid. It makes you human. Understanding it makes you harder to move without your awareness.

What comes next examines a different dimension of the same problem: not just how deliberate manipulators engineer belief, but how the source of information shapes what you're willing to believe before you've evaluated a single claim.

The badge matters more than most people realize, and more than most people want to admit.[14]

Chapter Summary

- Deliberate manipulation differs from accidental manipulation in one critical way: someone on the other side understands your psychological architecture and is using that understanding intentionally to produce conclusions you'll experience as your own.

- The most effective deliberate manipulation doesn't target your reasoning. It targets your identity, establishing who you are in relation to a community and a set of beliefs before presenting the claims those beliefs contain.

- Propaganda works by creating the subjective experience of clarity: the feeling of finally seeing what was always true. That feeling is the manipulation's most complete achievement and its most durable product.

- The patterns worth learning to notice: identity before evidence, emotional activation before content, manufactured consensus, and gradual escalation from credible claims toward positions you would have rejected at the outset.

- Knowledge of these mechanisms doesn't guarantee immunity. It changes the texture of the experience, creating the moment of pause between the feeling of clarity and the conclusion that feeling is trying to produce. That pause is where your thinking remains your own.

CHAPTER 7

The Badge, Not the Evidence

The Room That Deferred to the Wrong Voice

The Space Shuttle Challenger broke apart seventy-three seconds after launch on January 28, 1986. All seven crew members died. The Rogers Commission investigation that followed uncovered something that has since become a defining case study in organizational psychology and decision making failure.[1]

The night before the launch, engineers at Morton Thiokol raised serious concerns.[2] Roger Boisjoly and other engineers had documented evidence that the O-ring seals on the boosters performed poorly in cold temperatures. The launch was scheduled for an unusually cold Florida morning. Boisjoly and his colleagues argued clearly, with documented data, that the launch should be delayed.

NASA managers pushed back. The pressure to launch was significant. There had already been delays. The program needed momentum. A Thiokol manager named Joe Kilminster, facing that institutional pressure, asked his engineering team to take off their engineer hats and put on their management hats. The recommendation to delay was reversed. The launch proceeded.

The engineers in that room were not ignored because their evidence was weak. Their evidence was strong, and they presented it clearly. They were overridden because the authority structure of the situation, the institutional weight of NASA's expectations, the seniority of the managers involved, and the social pressure to align with those who held positional power, created conditions in which the badge outweighed the data.[3]

Roger Boisjoly knew the next morning what the outcome would be. He watched the launch from the ground. He was right about everything, and it changed nothing.

This is what authority bias costs when it operates at its most consequential.

The Shortcut That Usually Works and Sometimes Doesn't

Your brain developed the authority shortcut for good reasons. Evaluating every claim from experts in every area, across every decision you make in a day, is not possible. You can't independently verify your pharmacist's dosage instructions, your accountant's tax advice, or your mechanic's diagnosis. Deferring to people with relevant expertise and credentials is not a failure of critical thinking. It is a practical necessity.[4]

Your mind responds to the appearance of authority. Someone speaks to you with a confident tone, official branding, credentials displayed prominently, institutional affiliation, and the social consensus is that this person knows what they're talking about. You believe in their perceived status rather than the actual quality of their reasoning.

Those signals can be present without the substance that's supposed to justify them. They can also be deliberately manufactured, as an earlier chapter established, or they can be entirely genuine while still being wrong.

Boisjoly's managers had real authority. They held legitimate positions in a respected institution. The authority was not fabricated. It was real, and it was wrong. That distinction matters because it means authority bias doesn't require deception to cause harm. It requires only the ordinary human tendency to treat the source as evidence.

The Person Who Trusted the Right Source at the Wrong Moment

Daniel D. is fifty-one years old. He spent thirty years building a financial planning practice and considers himself, with good reason, a sophisticated evaluator of investment claims. He has seen market cycles, client panics, and no small number of confident predictions that turned out to be wrong.

Four years ago, Daniel attended a private investment briefing organized by a firm he respected. The presenter was a former senior figure at a major international financial institution. The credentials were real.

The presentation was polished, data rich, and delivered with the particular kind of confidence that said professional, not salesmanship. The investment opportunity presented was unconventional, but the reasoning was sophisticated. Daniel found himself less skeptical than he would have been with an unknown presenter. Any skepticism he felt was caution he was choosing to set aside in the presence of someone who clearly understood the landscape better than most.

He invested a significant amount. Eighteen months later, the investment had failed substantially. The presenter's credentials were genuine. The institutional affiliation was real. The confidence was authentic. Daniel had assumed the credentials guaranteed that the reasoning behind the recommendation was as sound as the presentation of it.

Daniel knew, abstractly, that credentialed people can be wrong. He had seen it many times. In that room, with that presenter, with that institutional weight behind the recommendation, his scrutiny had adjusted before the content arrived. The badge had done its work before the evidence had a chance to be examined.[5]

He describes the experience now not with bitterness but with a specific kind of clarity. "I knew he was credible," Daniel says. "I just confused credible with correct."

Psychologists call this the authority heuristic.[6] It operates automatically and below conscious awareness. You don't decide to believe the expert. You simply find yourself less skeptical, less inclined to probe, less likely to notice the gap between what's being claimed and what the evidence actually supports. The evaluation happens, but it happens differently, with less scrutiny, because the source has already done some of the work your critical thinking would otherwise do.

How Authority Shapes Evaluation Before Evaluation Begins

Daniel's experience illustrates something more precise than simple trust. Authority bias doesn't operate by making you abandon evaluation. It operates by adjusting the evaluation before it begins. The question shifts from "Is this claim well supported?" to "Does this claim fit with what I'd expect from someone of this caliber?" Those are different questions and they produce different levels of scrutiny.[7]

This adjustment happens in both directions. When a source carries authority, claims that would otherwise feel questionable feel plausible. When a source lacks authority, claims that are well supported can feel less convincing simply because of who's presenting them. The same data, delivered by a graduate student and a named professor, receives different levels of automatic credibility. The same medical recommendation, delivered by a general practitioner and a specialist, carries different weight. The content is identical. The badge changes the reception.[8]

Deliberate manipulation exploits this mechanism directly. An earlier chapter examined how authority cues, expert language, official branding, confident presentation, and the phrase "a former official confirms," are used to manufacture the feeling of credibility rather than demonstrate it. Borrowed certainty is when the claim borrows the credibility of the source without the source's credibility being relevant to whether the claim is actually true.[9]

The sophistication of the exploitation is worth noting. Deliberate authority manipulation doesn't require false credentials. It requires only the right signals, the right tone, the right vocabulary, the right institutional framing, and the right social context in which those signals are accepted. Boisjoly's managers didn't fake their authority. They deliberately chose to support decisions that were not sound.

When the Source Becomes the Argument

Critical thinking requires that you learn to recognize the moment when you find yourself evaluating a claim primarily by asking who said it rather than what they said.

Is the reasoning sound?

Is this person someone whose reasoning you trust?

Does the evidence support the conclusion?

Would someone of this credibility attach themselves to a false conclusion?

These aren't irrational questions. Credibility is real and relevant. The problem arrives when source evaluation replaces content evaluation.

A cardiologist's authority in cardiology does not extend automatically to their investment advice. A decorated general's authority in military strategy does not extend automatically to foreign policy analysis. A celebrated economist's authority in macroeconomics does not extend automatically to their views on educational policy. Credentials are domain specific. Authority bias treats them as general.[10]

What You Can Do With This

When you find yourself persuaded by a source, pause long enough to ask whether you're persuaded by the argument or by who's making it. Ask whether the source's credibility is actually relevant to the specific claim being made.

Those are different things and they require different responses. Being persuaded by a credible argument from a credible source is exactly how good thinking works. Being persuaded by the source before you've evaluated the argument is the authority bias shortcut at work.

A few specific practices help interrupt the shortcut without eliminating the useful version of it.

Look for the argument beneath the authority. Even when a source is genuinely credible, the reasoning behind their claim should be available and examinable. "Trust me, I know this field" is not an argument. It's an invitation to skip the argument. Credible sources with sound reasoning don't resist having their reasoning examined.

Notice the social context. Authority bias intensifies in rooms, in groups, and in institutional settings where the weight of consensus and hierarchy is present.[11] The same claim you'd scrutinize carefully in a casual conversation can feel more settled in a formal presentation. That feeling is the social amplification of authority, not additional evidence for the claim.

The clarifying question to carry into any high stakes evaluation is simply this, are you evaluating the claim, or are you evaluating the person making it?

What the Badge Costs When You Forget It's Just a Badge

Roger Boisjoly spent the years after Challenger testifying, writing, and speaking about what happened in that room the night before the launch. He wasn't bitter in his public accounts. He was precise.

He described the moment the recommendation was reversed not as a moment of corruption but as a moment of ordinary institutional deference. The people in that room were not bad. They were responding to authority in the way authority tends to make people respond.

Daniel made a version of the same error at a smaller scale with smaller consequences. He confused credible with correct. He recovered financially over time. He describes himself as a genuinely better evaluator now, not because he trusts less but because he's learned to hold the authority signal and the content evaluation separately, to let the source guide his attention without replacing his judgment.

Both stories point to the same place. The credentials of the authority figure hold real information. They tell you something worth knowing about where a claim is coming from and what kind of expertise is behind it. They don't tell you whether the claim is true.

We believe the badge because the badge usually points toward something worth believing. The discipline is remembering that "usually" and "always" are not the same thing. The badge is evidence. It was never meant to be a verdict.

What comes next examines how the very words used to frame a claim shape what conclusions feel available before the argument has even begun. It's the invisible architecture of language that determines not just how you describe reality but what you're able to perceive within it.[12]

Chapter Summary

- Authority bias is the tendency to evaluate claims based on the credibility of their source rather than the quality of the reasoning behind them. The shortcut is necessary and usually useful. It becomes costly when source evaluation replaces rather than informs content evaluation.

- The authority heuristic operates automatically and below conscious awareness. It adjusts your level of scrutiny before evaluation begins, making claims from high authority sources feel more plausible and claims from low authority sources feel less convincing, regardless of the content's actual quality.

- Credentials are domain specific. Authority bias treats them as general. A source's expertise in one field does not extend automatically to claims made in another, and the brain doesn't always make that distinction without deliberate effort.

- Borrowed certainty is the deliberate exploitation of authority signals: confident tone, official framing, expert language, and institutional affiliation used to manufacture credibility for claims that haven't earned it through reasoning.

- The discipline is holding the badge and the argument separately. Let the source inform your attention. Don't let it replace your judgment. The question worth asking is not whether this person is credible. It's whether this specific argument, from this specific person, in this specific domain, has earned the credibility it's borrowing.

CHAPTER 8

Can I Still Trust Myself?

The Woman Who Couldn't Outrun Her Own Byline

Miriam spent eleven years as a science journalist. She was known for getting things right. She traced studies back to the original data, called researchers directly, and held stories until the sourcing felt airtight. When something felt off, people went to her.

For almost four years she wrote enthusiastically about a popular nutrition framework. Then the bottom fell out. The research behind it had been discredited. Her first reaction was not embarrassment. It was that dizzy feeling like the floor moved.

She had written fourteen long pieces. She had praised the framework in a book proposal. She had even dismissed a researcher who raised concerns, calling him contrarian in print. This belief did not sneak in.

She carried it in and displayed it.

What came next was not a clean correction. It was a long inner argument she could not settle. She replayed the evidence at two in the morning. She reread her own work and felt her stomach tighten. Sure, every journalist gets something wrong. She could accept that.

But a bigger question sat underneath it.

If her process led her here, what else had it led her to that she had not caught yet?

The hardest part was not the mistake. It was what the mistake did to her confidence in her own judgment.

Two Wounds, Not One

When people realize they were seriously misled, two things usually hit at the same time. Most people treat them like one problem, but they are not.

The first is the factual correction. A belief was wrong. Now you know it was wrong. It feels bad, but it is simple. Old information gets replaced.

The second is harder. You stop looking at the belief and you start looking at yourself. You ask how the belief got in. You ask what that says about your mind. This is where self trust can get shaken.

Miriam was not only revising a nutrition framework. She was looking back at a version of herself who sounded confident and public and certain, and now that memory felt dangerous. She was not only asking, Was the framework true. She was asking, Can I trust my judgment at all. That question is harder, and it rarely has a clean answer.

Psychologists who study identity disruption see a pattern here. When a person ties their identity to competence, being wrong can feel like a threat to who they are, not just a correction of a fact. Experts and professionals often react this way. The emotional impact does not match the size of the error because it is not really about the error. It is about the gap between who they believed they were and the evidence now in front of them.[1]

That gap is real. It deserves respect. But it also gets misread. People treat it as proof they cannot trust themselves, and that misunderstanding can do more harm than the original mistake.

What Being Wrong Doesn't Mean

Being wrong in a complex information world does not mean your thinking is broken. It means you were thinking inside a world full of messages built to persuade, repeated storylines, identity pressure, and emotional cues. That is the world this book has been describing. The mechanisms that shaped your belief are not signs of a defective mind. They are signs of a human one.[2]

Miriam did not fail because she was careless. She got pulled into a familiar sequence. A framework arrived wearing scientific language. It was carried by voices with institutional credibility. It showed up everywhere. It started to feel established before she ever consciously chose it.[3] Her intelligence did not protect her. It helped her explain the framework well, defend it publicly, and dismiss objections.[4] That is not stupidity. That is the pattern we started with in the opening chapter.

The danger is not learning you were wrong. The danger is what you decide being wrong means about you.

Two common reactions show up.

One is quick replacement. The old belief collapses and a new strong belief rushes in to take its place. Certainty returns faster than the evidence supports because certainty feels steady and the mind wants relief.[5]

The other is retreat. Everything feels questionable. Every source feels unreliable. You stop committing to conclusions because commitment feels like exposure.

Both reactions make sense. Neither is accurate.

A better definition of self trust is not, I am always right. A better definition is, I can correct myself. Those are built on different foundations. The first one collapses the moment it meets a serious mistake. The second one grows stronger each time you practice it.

The Ground Beneath the Error

It took Miriam about eight months to feel steady again. It was not a straight line. Looking back, she could name three shifts that helped.

First was separating herself from her conclusions.

That can sound abstract until you live it.

Miriam saw herself as someone whose beliefs were well founded. That was part of her professional identity. When a belief turned out wrong, it did not feel like a normal error. It felt like a verdict on her as a person. The work was learning to stop treating a wrong conclusion as proof of a flawed self.

Her identity was not her conclusions. Her identity was the values she brought to forming them: care, rigor, and a willingness to follow evidence. Those values had not disappeared. She had been operating inside a world that rewards repetition and authority, and every mind has limits when those forces are turned up. That is the difference between a mistake that humiliates and a mistake that teaches.

Psychologists who study how people respond to threatening information have found something important: when people feel secure in their core values, they become more open to evidence that challenges what they believe. Security does not make them sloppy. It makes them less defended, which means the evidence can actually land.[6] Miriam found this to be true. Once she stopped treating the error as a character flaw, she could look at how the belief formed without flinching. That is what helped her build a stronger process going forward.

Second was treating revision as part of the job, not proof she was incompetent.

She had not been pretending to be rigorous. She had been rigorous within the limits of what she knew to look for. Now she could see those limits. That was information, not indictment.

She started framing it the way she would frame a correction in journalism. Not as failure, but as the work doing what it is supposed to do: staying accountable to new facts. Inside her mind, the story shifted from I was wrong to I updated. Those are not the same. One sounds like a verdict. The other sounds like a process still alive.

Those first two shifts mattered. But the third one is the most durable, and it is where this chapter has been going.

The Question That Stays Stable

Conclusions are fragile. They depend on what you know at a particular moment, and what you know can change. Confidence that depends on never changing your conclusion is confidence built on something that will eventually crack.

Process is different. Process is how you think. It is not the answer you give, it is the habits that get you there. Miriam started to define her process with simple habits: slow down before forming strong opinions, look for what would change your mind, separate what you know from what you inferred, notice what you absorbed through repetition, and be willing to say I am not sure yet even when certainty is rewarded.[7]

When confidence is grounded in process, changing your mind does not feel like losing yourself. It feels like the system working. A scientist whose new data contradicts a hypothesis does not lose faith in science. They trust the method. The strength is in testing, not in never being wrong.

Miriam put it simply. She stopped asking, Can I trust my conclusions. She started asking, Can I trust how I arrive at conclusions. That second question stays steady even when specific answers change. It gives your mind somewhere solid to stand without requiring perfection.

It also changes what it feels like to be challenged. When your confidence is tied to a conclusion, a challenge can feel like a threat. You defend because the alternative feels like collapse. When your confidence is tied to a process, a challenge becomes useful input. You can engage because engaging is the process working. You are not defending a position. You are testing your method.

The Calibration Point

Miriam had to move through something uncomfortable before she could correct the record publicly.

Doubt showed up, and at first it was helpful. It slowed her down. It reduced overconfidence. It created space for questions. She questioned sources more carefully. She looked harder at how claims were built. She added friction where she used to move fast.

But doubt has another form too. That version does not sharpen thinking. It goes after the thinker.

The difference is what the skepticism is aimed at. Healthy doubt questions conclusions. The kind that paralyzes questions competence. Let me examine this more carefully is healthy. I cannot trust my own judgment is something else.[8]

A compass does not become useless because you misread it once. It becomes more valuable when you learn to read it better. The same is true of a mind. Learning that repetition, manipulation, or identity pressure shaped your thinking does not mean your mind is broken. It means you can now see the forces that bend it. That insight helps you protect yourself next time.

Extreme self distrust can even feel like virtue. It can feel like humility. But humility does not require erasing yourself. You can admit real limits without destroying the confidence you need to function.

Balanced thinking needs two things together: openness and stability. Openness allows revision. Stability allows decisions. The goal is not to get rid of doubt. The goal is to set it to the right level.

Miriam found her calibration point about six months in. She learned to tell the difference between the discomfort that says, Look closer, and the discomfort that says, You are a fraud. The first is useful. The second is distraction. They can feel similar. They are not.

What She Wrote Anyway

There was a part of Miriam's situation nobody wants to talk about directly. She was wrong in public. The articles existed. The dismissal of the dissenting researcher existed, under her name. Fixing the record meant doing it visibly, and visible correction carries real social cost.

Research on commitment and consistency shows that people are strongly motivated to appear consistent with their prior public statements.[9] Consistency signals reliability. Certainty is rewarded in many environments, and updating can be read as weakness. So people double down privately, soften quietly without admitting the shift, or go silent.[10] None of that produces the honest correction the situation requires.

The fear is not irrational. Changing your mind publicly, especially after arguing strongly, can change how people see you. The question is what kind of status you are trying to protect, and whether it is worth more than accuracy.

Miriam knew some colleagues would see the correction as proof she had lost her edge. That risk was real, and she knew it before she wrote a word. But status built on rigid certainty is fragile. It requires you to defend everything you said before, which turns your past positions into something you must constantly maintain, even when it costs you truth.

She wrote the correction anyway. She named the researcher she dismissed and admitted his concerns were warranted. The piece ran. Several colleagues she respected responded with something closer to admiration than sympathy. They did not admire the mistake. They admired the clarity and directness of the correction. A few sources who had been reluctant to work with her started returning her calls. The status she feared losing was more durable than the certainty she was protecting.

That will not always be the outcome. Some environments do punish revision. But the credibility offered in those environments is rarely worth what it costs to keep.

The Drift That Locks Beliefs in Place

Looking back, Miriam noticed something subtle. Her language changed.

She stopped writing, the evidence suggests, and started writing, we know. Absolute language does not only communicate certainty. It builds certainty inside you. If you say this is established fact enough times, your mind starts treating it that way, even when the evidence is thinner than the language implies.

Provisional language works differently. Phrases like based on what I currently understand or this is where the evidence seems to point create a small space between you and your conclusion. That space makes updating easier. You can hold the conclusion firmly enough to act, and loosely enough to release it when the evidence changes.[11]

This is about internal accuracy. It is about being honest with yourself about what you know, what you suspect, and what you are repeating because you have heard it so often. Most beliefs are not certainties. They are the best available interpretations of incomplete information.

Language that reflects that reality is more honest. And being honest about what you truly know and do not know makes you harder to manipulate. It is harder to engineer false certainty in someone who keeps that distinction clear.

What Consistency Actually Demands

Consistency has a better reputation than it deserves.

Culturally, we praise people who stand by their beliefs and distrust people who change their minds.

We often treat updating as a character flaw. But there is a distinction many people miss: integrity and rigidity are not the same.

Integrity means your values stay stable. Rigidity means your conclusions never change. Those lead to very different behavior. A person with integrity follows evidence wherever it leads, even when it is uncomfortable. A rigid person defends prior positions because changing feels like incoherence. One produces clearer thinking over time. The other produces a growing pile of defended beliefs that becomes more expensive to maintain every year.[12]

Real consistency is not holding the same opinion forever. It is applying the same honest standard of evaluation over time. If your standard is, I update when credible evidence warrants it, then changing your mind is the consistent move.

The comparison that matters is not between someone who never changed and someone who changed twice. The comparison is between someone who changed for good reasons and someone who changed because the social wind shifted. Your method is what separates them. The outcome cannot.

Miriam eventually wrote a short piece about the whole experience. She kept it precise, not confessional, not dramatic. She described what she believed, what changed, and how she was thinking about her process going forward.

The response surprised her. People who had followed her work for years said it was among the most useful things she had written, not because it contained new facts, but because it showed something rare: a thinker being accountable to evidence while still sounding like herself.

That recognition, that a mind revising itself is a mind working correctly, usually arrives quietly. It does not feel like a revelation. It feels like permission.

Changing your mind does not mean losing yourself. It means proving the part of you worth trusting is still working: the part that follows evidence, tolerates uncertainty, and stays honest about limits. A mind that can revise is more reliable than a mind that cannot. People who understand that do not experience revision as defeat. They experience it as the point.

What comes next examines the mind's automatic mode, how it mistakes speed for accuracy, and why the information environment you navigate every day is designed to keep you from noticing the difference.[13]

Chapter Summary

- Most people who discover they were seriously wrong experience two things at once and treat them as one. The first is factual correction. The second is the more unsettling look at the process that produced the belief. The second is what can shake self trust, and it is what requires the most care.

- Being wrong in a complex information environment is not proof of defective thinking. It is human thinking operating inside systems built to exploit ordinary tendencies.

- When people confuse these two experiences, they either rebuild certainty too quickly or retreat into paralyzing self skepticism. Neither response is accurate.

- Trust built on being right all the time collapses after the first serious mistake. Trust built on the ability to correct and update, and to stay honest about limits, is the kind that endures.

- You are not your beliefs. You are the thinker who holds them. When identity is rooted in values like intellectual honesty and genuine curiosity rather than fixed positions, revision strengthens the self instead of threatening it.

- Confidence moved from conclusions to process is confidence that survives new evidence.

- Healthy doubt sharpens thinking by questioning conclusions. The paralyzing version attacks competence and can disguise itself as humility while causing real harm. Learning to tell the difference is a key skill for any careful thinker.

- Changing your mind publicly can carry real social cost. The status worth protecting is built on intellectual honesty, not on the appearance of never being wrong.

- True consistency is not defending the same conclusion forever. It is applying the same honest standard of evaluation no matter where the evidence leads.

- A mind that can revise is not weaker. It is a mind still working correctly.

CHAPTER 9

Slowing Down Your Thinking

The Verdict That Arrived Before the Evidence

Owen had been a senior editor at a regional news outlet for sixteen years. He was good at it. Younger reporters trusted him with hard calls about what to publish, what to hold, and what needed one more round of checking. He built that reputation slowly.

Then a story broke on a Tuesday afternoon in September, and he published it in eleven minutes.

The claim was serious: a local official had allegedly steered public funds to a contractor with a personal connection. A source Owen knew sent a message with what looked like a supporting document. The story fit a pattern Owen had been watching. That morning's editorial meeting had already primed the topic. By the time the message arrived, everything in the room felt aligned: this is real, this matters, this needs to run now.

He did not verify the document. He did not call the official. He told himself there was no time.

The story ran. By Thursday, the document had been shown to be altered. The official issued a statement. Owen's outlet ran a correction that drew more attention than the original piece. Two junior reporters on his team fielded angry calls for a week.

On Friday morning, Owen tried to replay what happened inside his mind on Tuesday. He had not been reckless or lazy. He had been confident. That confidence felt like certainty. The certainty felt like evidence. And when the real evidence finally arrived, it was too late to separate it from the conclusion he had already published.

Why Fast Feels Like Accurate

What happened to Owen has a name and a well studied mechanism. Daniel Kahneman described two broad modes of thinking that operate differently and serve different purposes.[1] One mode is fast, automatic, pattern driven, and emotionally responsive. The other is slower, more deliberate, more effortful, and more accurate when accuracy is what the moment demands. Owen's eleven minutes were almost entirely the first kind. He never really entered the second.

Fast thinking is useful. It handles thousands of small decisions each day. Slow thinking is for higher stakes moments when the evidence is unclear. The problem is not that fast thinking exists. The problem is that fast thinking can feel exactly like careful thinking from the inside.

Owen did not experience himself as skipping steps. He experienced himself as recognizing something true. The pattern matched. The source was familiar. The context felt known. His mind produced a conclusion and wrapped it in the feeling of certainty, and that feeling can be indistinguishable from the feeling he gets when he has done the work properly.[2]

This is the central deception of automatic thinking. It does not announce itself. It does not arrive feeling like a shortcut. It arrives feeling like clarity.

Speed and accuracy are different. Speed is how quickly a conclusion forms. Accuracy is whether it is correct. The mind often mixes them up because in ordinary life the fast conclusion is usually good enough. You do not verify that a chair will hold you before sitting down. But the same system that handles chairs also handles contested claims, political information, and emotionally charged narratives. It does not calibrate itself to complexity. It calibrates itself to familiarity. Familiarity has nothing to do with truth.[3]

What Emotion Does to the Clock

When Owen reconstructed the sequence honestly, he noticed something else. He had wanted the story to be true. Not cynically. Not as a lie. He had been frustrated with the official before. The document seemed to confirm a pattern Owen had suspected for months. When the message arrived, the feeling was not just interest. It was vindication.

Researchers who study emotion and cognition have found that strong emotional states narrow what the mind considers. Anger makes threats look larger. Fear makes dangers look closer. Moral outrage makes action feel urgent. Vindication makes evidence look conclusive.[4] That is what happened to Owen. Emotion did not just color his conclusion. It shaped what information reached evaluation at all. Details that supported his interpretation became vivid. Details that complicated it faded.

Owen noticed the supporting document. He did not notice the formatting inconsistency in the header that the verification editor caught two days later. Both were visible. Only one registered.

Strong emotion also changes the experience of time. When emotion runs high, uncertainty feels harder to tolerate. Holding a claim open and sitting with I do not know yet can feel unbearable. The pressure to close the loop increases. The relief of closing it, of reaching a conclusion and moving toward action, gets misread as correctness.[5] The feeling of resolution can masquerade as the feeling of accuracy.

Later, Owen reduced it to three steps: it felt urgent, urgency felt like importance, and importance felt like justification. Each step felt solid. None of them were actually connected to whether the document was real.

The Space Between Stimulus and Response

There is a version of this story where Owen pauses for thirty minutes before publishing.

He calls the official's office. He sends the document to the outlet's legal contact. He asks a colleague to check the formatting. None of this is special. It is the procedure he would teach a new hire. He knew how to do it. The knowledge was intact.

What was missing was not competence. What was missing was friction, the moment that would have activated the competence he already had.

That is what slowing down means in practice. It is not learning new skills. It is inserting a gap between stimulus and response. The gap does not need to be long. Owen's normal process, applied properly, would have taken under an hour. What it required was a choice, conscious or habitual, to treat the feeling of certainty as a signal to check rather than a signal to publish.

The mind does not make that choice automatically. The default is to treat certainty as confirmation. Changing the default requires a habit that runs in moments of high emotion and high confidence. Those are exactly the moments when the habit is hardest to execute.

The good news is that the habit does not require overriding the fast conclusion. It only requires delaying commitment. Owen could have felt certain and still made the call. He could have felt vindicated and still sent the document to legal. The emotion did not have to vanish. It just had to stop being the final voice.

Researchers who study how people interrupt automatic responses have found that the most effective friction is not a long checklist. It is a single question applied at the moment of highest confidence: what would I need to see to conclude I am wrong about this?[6]

Owen knew what the answer would have been: a document that holds up under scrutiny, a corroborating source, a call to the official that does not produce a clean denial. None of those checks take long. All of them require asking the question first. The question gets asked when certainty triggers curiosity rather than action.

It also matters to be clear about what this is and is not. Fast thinking has real value. It handles huge amounts of information efficiently and draws on experience. Gary Klein studied expert decisions under pressure and found that experienced practitioners often reach good conclusions quickly by recognizing patterns built from deep relevant knowledge.[7]

Owen had that kind of experience. Sixteen years of editorial work gave him real instincts about sources, documents, and official statements. Those instincts had served him well many times. On that Tuesday, he reached for those instincts and found something else in their place. The problem was not fast instincts. The problem was treating them as complete. The emotional context quietly displaced his experience as the true source of his certainty.

The goal is not to slow down every thought. The goal is to notice when fast thinking is running on emotional fuel rather than genuine depth, and to pause long enough for a key question to surface: is the certainty I feel coming from what I know, or from what I want to be true?

Owen cannot always answer that perfectly in the moment. Neither can anyone. He now waits at least forty minutes before publishing anything that arrives with the feeling of immediate obviousness, not because the feeling is always wrong, but because it has been wrong often enough that the pause costs less than the alternative.

The Information Environment That Works Against You

The modern information environment and fast thinking fit together too well. That alignment is not accidental. Headlines are built to trigger immediate emotion. Short video clips are engineered for snap judgment. Social feeds move fast enough that slowing down feels like falling behind.

The environment rewards rapid engagement and punishes hesitation. Platforms amplify content that provokes strong reaction because strong reaction produces the behavior the platform is designed to maximize: sharing, commenting, staying.[8]

Information now moves at a pace that bypasses deliberate evaluation. An emotionally resonant claim, repeated across multiple feeds by sources that feel familiar and credible, builds the same false familiarity described earlier.[9]

The repetition is faster than it used to be. The emotional triggers are more precisely tuned. Words like urgent, obvious, everyone knows are chosen to close the loop before evaluation begins.[10] Social proof, the sense that many people already treat something as true, can arrive before most people have examined the claim at all.[11]

Owen's newsroom was not a social media feed, but the pressure worked the same way: emotional charge, a familiar pattern, apparent confirmation from a trusted source, and the sense that others were already moving. The room had its own urgency. Owen absorbed it without noticing he had absorbed it.

The awareness that matters is not abstract awareness of bias or incentives. It is the personal awareness of what the environment is doing to your internal state right now. When you feel urgency but cannot name its source, examine it. When something feels obvious before you have examined the evidence, that gap is exactly where deliberate slowing belongs.

Owen still works as an editor. He is better at the job now, not because he is faster or more confident, but because he treats immediate certainty the way a careful driver treats a green light at a blind intersection: it is permission to go, but it is still worth a second look.

What Comes After Noticing

The practical question is not whether to slow down. It is what slowing down looks like inside a moment that is moving fast.

It does not require the absence of emotion or the suspension of instinct. It is a question asked when certainty feels loudest: where is this certainty coming from? Not as an accusation. Not as proof the conclusion is wrong. As a real check on the difference between certainty earned and certainty felt.

Owen asks it now. Not perfectly. Not in time every time. Often enough that his track record is different. He treats conviction as a clue rather than a conclusion. The stronger the conviction, the more carefully he looks at what produced it. The more obvious something seems, the more he wants to know why it seems obvious.

He also added one specific practice after the correction. When a story arrives feeling urgent, he writes down what he expects to find before he verifies anything. He does not do this to bury himself in procedure. He does it to make the expectation visible and separate from what the evidence actually shows.

The gap between the two is where he now does his most careful work.

That instinct, to question certainty rather than ride it, runs against an environment built to make you react. It takes practice, and the practice compounds. Over time, the mind that slows down often enough develops a feel for when pausing is warranted. That is its own kind of fast thinking, not automatic, but earned.

What comes next examines something that operates even earlier than the moment of reaction: the specific words chosen to describe a claim before it reaches you, and how that framing shapes what conclusions feel available before you have evaluated a single fact.

Chapter Summary

- Fast thinking is automatic, pattern driven, and emotionally responsive. It handles most of what the mind encounters efficiently and usually well.
- The problem is not fast thinking. The problem is that from the inside it can be hard to distinguish fast thinking from accurate thinking. Both feel like certainty. Only one requires evidence to get there.
- Emotion accelerates the fast mode. Vindication, outrage, urgency, and fear narrow what the mind considers and compress the felt need to hold a claim open. The relief of reaching a conclusion can be misread as proof it is accurate.

- Slowing down does not mean eliminating fast thinking or overriding instinct. It means inserting friction at the point of highest confidence: a question that asks where certainty is coming from before treating it as a reason to act.

- The modern information environment is built to bypass that friction. It moves at the pace of automatic reaction. Content is engineered to provoke emotion before evaluation begins. Familiarity that accumulates through repetition and apparent social consensus can produce a feeling of truth before any evidence has been examined.

- Expertise can make fast thinking more reliable, but it does not remove vulnerability. Expert pattern recognition built from genuine experience is different from confidence borrowed from emotional context. The difference is not visible in the moment. It is visible in the outcome.

- The habit worth building is not patience. It is sensitivity to notice when certainty arrived before the evidence did, and to pause long enough to ask whether that order matters. It usually does.

CHAPTER 10

Talking to Others Without Becoming the Enemy

The Conversation That Wasn't Supposed to Go That Way

Carla had done this before, hundreds of times. She was a family mediator with twenty years of experience. Her work was built on a simple belief: most conflicts can be resolved if the conditions are right. She had sat with divorcing couples, estranged siblings, and business partners turned adversaries. She knew how to hold a room.

The conversation with her brother at Thanksgiving was not a room she could hold.

They had not seen each other in fourteen months.

They had been close once, the kind of close that makes adult distance feel like a betrayal. The distance started around the same time their political views stopped overlapping. Neither of them named the drift while it was happening. Then Thanksgiving arrived, and her brother made a casual remark about a policy Carla cared about. It cut through her professional composure like it was never there.

She heard herself answer with a sharpness she did not mean to use. He matched it. The table went quiet. Within four minutes they were not talking about the policy. They were talking about who the other person had become.

Carla drove home replaying it. She had said the right words in the wrong tone. She had stated facts he already knew. She had made arguments she could write in her sleep. None of it landed, and she knew why, because she teaches this for a living.

What stopped her was not ignorance. She had the tools. She was just not protected from the situation itself.

Why Debates Don't Work and Arguments Don't Either

When people disagree with someone they care about, they usually reach for the same tool: a better argument.

They gather evidence. They prepare counterpoints. They look for the flaw in the other person's position and lay it out clearly. That approach works only in a narrow setting: when both people agree the goal is accuracy, and both agree to be persuaded by evidence.

That is not what most real conversations are like.

Psychologist Ziva Kunda studied motivated reasoning, the tendency to evaluate evidence in the direction of a conclusion the mind already wants to protect.[1] She found a consistent pattern: people scrutinize arguments that challenge their beliefs more aggressively than arguments that support them.

The standard changes depending on the direction. Supporting arguments get waved through. Challenging arguments get searched for flaws.

So when you present a better argument to someone who is emotionally invested, you do not get neutral evaluation. You get defense. The argument feels like a threat, and the mind does not calmly weigh threats. It tries to neutralize them.[2]

Carla knew this. She had explained it to clients many times. She knew her brother was not going to weigh her evidence and update his position at the dinner table. She knew that the sharper she got, the harder he would hold his ground.

She went there anyway, not because she forgot the mechanism, but because knowing how it works is not the same as being insulated from it.

The emotional regulation that good conversation requires does not fade slowly as stakes rise. It can collapse at a threshold. That threshold shows up when the other person is someone whose opinion of you connects to your own sense of worth.[3] Carla could hold a room of strangers at that edge. Her brother was on the other side of it.

Her mistake was not intellectual. It was the assumption that this time would be different. That if her argument was clear enough, the relationship would absorb it. Neither was true.

What the Argument Was Actually About

The next morning Carla replayed the conversation and noticed something she missed in the moment.

Her brother was not really arguing about the policy.

He was arguing about whether people like him, people with his values, people from where they came from, deserve to be taken seriously. The policy was the surface. Under it was something older: the feeling that his world gets dismissed by people who consider themselves thoughtful. Carla, his sister and a professional mediator, felt like the closest representative of that dismissal.

Carla was not only talking about the policy either. She was defending a version of herself: someone educated, clear thinking, and competent. Her brother's position felt like evidence that someone she loved had been misled. She felt responsible, and responsibility can turn into urgency fast.

Jonathan Haidt has described moral foundations, the deep concerns that shape values and political judgment, including care, fairness, loyalty, authority, and sanctity.[4] His research suggests that people across ideological lines rarely disagree about whether these values matter. They disagree about how to weight them and which threats feel most urgent.[5]

Two people can argue fiercely about a policy while protecting the same underlying values through different threat perceptions.

Carla and her brother both cared about the same community. They grew up in it together. The policy affected that community, and each believed the other position would harm it. They were not enemies with opposite values. They were protective of the same thing and could not hear it in each other.

The Thing That Lowers the Temperature

Three days later Carla called her brother. She did not call to restart the argument, and she did not call to apologize for her position.

She spent those three days doing something she teaches others to do: trying to see his view from the inside, not to find the flaw, not to prepare a rebuttal, but to understand what it was protecting.

Even then, the call was hard. She sat with her phone for twenty minutes before dialing. She had helped other people through conversations like this for two decades, and her own hands still hesitated.

When he answered, she said, I think I understand why that matters to you. I do not think I showed that.

He was quiet. Then he said he did not think he showed it either.

Those words did what forty minutes at Thanksgiving did not. They did not change positions. They did not solve the policy question. But they named what had been missing: that his view came from something real, and she could see it.

The tone shifted. He said things he did not say at the table. So did she. The loud argument about policy had been covering a quieter one. The quieter one needed air.

He shared concerns he had never raised. She asked questions she had never thought to ask. Neither changed position, but both changed what they understood about what the other position was trying to protect.

Researchers who study belief change and belief stability find a pattern in conversations like this. People rarely revise a position when they feel their underlying concern has been dismissed. They sometimes revise when they feel it has been genuinely heard. The sequence matters more than the content.

Acknowledgment has to come before challenge. If challenge arrives first, it registers as an attack on the value itself, not a question about the reasoning. If acknowledgment comes first, challenge can land as a question.[6]

Carla had watched this in her work for years. She had watched couples move from contempt to conversation when one person stopped trying to win and started trying to understand. She had also watched the same conversation fail when understanding was performed rather than real.

The difference is not technique. It is whether curiosity is genuine. People can tell when you want to understand and when you are waiting for an opening.[7] The tells are small: how you listen, whether your questions go deeper, and whether you seem changed at all by what you heard.

Carla's call worked because she meant it. Her acknowledgment was not strategic. It came from real thought after she stopped trying to win.

The Surface and What's Beneath It

Over the next few weeks, the conversations looked different.

Carla did not abandon her position. She did not pretend his arguments suddenly convinced her. What she did was separate two things she had blended at Thanksgiving: disagreement with his conclusion and dismissal of the concern that produced it.

Those are different. A person can have a wrong conclusion, or a poorly supported one, while still protecting something real. A wrong conclusion does not erase the underlying concern. Treating it as if it does ends conversations, because it communicates more than disagreement. It communicates that the person's whole orientation is illegitimate.[8]

Most people can accept being wrong about a fact. Almost no one can accept being told that what they were trying to protect was not worth protecting.

Carla started asking questions she had never asked, not to gather ammunition, but because she realized she did not fully understand the shape of his view. She knew his policy position. She did not know what he feared would happen if she was right. She did not know what he thought the policy cost people he knew. She did not know what he had seen that made it feel urgent.

Some of what she heard surprised her. Some concerns were ones she shared, expressed through a framework she still found less convincing. Some positions still seemed factually mistaken to her. But the conversation changed shape. It became less about winning and more about comparing notes on how to protect the same place they came from.

Her position did not change. Neither did his, entirely. But something else shifted: the sense that the other person was the problem. That shift was what made conversation possible again.

The Distance That Wasn't There

What happened next mattered less than what it revealed about the mechanism underneath.

For years Carla assumed the distance between them was ideological, that their values had diverged. Once the argument stopped being performance, she found the values were mostly intact.

What diverged was what each of them believed was threatening those values most urgently. That is a different kind of disagreement. It is empirical, not moral. It is about what the world is like, not what should matter.

Empirical disagreements can be resolved with evidence. But not while both people are defending themselves.

Carla describes the change as a shift in who she thought she was talking to. She went to Thanksgiving thinking she was talking to someone with a wrong conclusion. She left thinking she was talking to a different person. Three days later she called once she realized she had been wrong about that too.

When you enter a disagreement looking for the shared value beneath the opposing view, you do not surrender your own position. You gain access to a conversation the other person can actually tolerate. If you enter as if the goal is to win, you close that access. Positions harden. Relationships strain. Everyone leaves more certain than they arrived.

Carla now uses Thanksgiving as a teaching story. Not because of what went wrong, but because of what the days after revealed. She spent forty minutes arguing with a version of her brother she constructed rather than the one sitting across from her. That constructed version was the main obstacle to the conversation they needed.

What Changes and What Doesn't

Understanding the emotional stakes under a disagreement does not guarantee minds will change.

Some beliefs carry strong identity investment. Some settings, especially public ones with an audience, make acknowledgment feel like surrender. Some conversations are not ready yet, and forcing them creates damage instead of progress.

What does change, reliably, is the quality of connection. When both people feel their underlying concerns are present rather than dismissed, the conversation is more likely to stay in reasoning instead of dropping into identity defense. It is more likely to produce real uncertainty, the kind that leaves room to revisit later even if no one changes position today.

The shift Carla made, from winning to understanding, did not change her brother's mind about the policy in the short term. It changed what kind of conversation was available to them. What became available was a conversation where both could speak honestly, instead of speaking to defend what they already said.

That is not small. It is the difference between a relationship that survives disagreement and one that hardens around it.

What comes next examines the bond that forms when people connect through shared opposition rather than shared values, why that bond can feel like depth when it is not, and why the same mechanism that deepens division can sometimes create unexpected common ground.[9]

Chapter Summary

- Most disagreements are not really about facts. They are about what the facts represent: threats to identity, security, fairness, or belonging. The argument you hear is often not the argument that matters.

- Motivated reasoning means a better argument can produce more resistance, not less. The mind does not neutrally evaluate challenges to emotionally invested beliefs. It defends against them.[1, 2]

- Opposing positions often share a value underneath. People can protect the same concern through different threat perceptions. Many big political fights are empirical disagreements about what is happening, not moral disagreements about what should matter.[4, 5]

- Acknowledgment must come before challenge. A challenge before acknowledgment feels like an attack on the value. A challenge after genuine acknowledgment can be heard as a question.[6]

- Curiosity has to be real. People can detect performed understanding, and it triggers the same defenses as direct attack.[7]

- You can understand what someone is protecting without abandoning your position. The key is separating disagreement with a conclusion from dismissal of the concern beneath it.[8]

- When you look for shared values beneath an opposing view, you do not give up your own view. You gain access to a conversation the other person can actually have.

CHAPTER 11

Common Enemy Intimacy

The Bond That Forms in the Dark

There's a particular kind of closeness that forms quickly between people. It doesn't require vulnerability. It doesn't require shared history or hard won trust. It doesn't ask anything of the people involved except agreement about who or what is wrong. It arrives fast, it feels warm, and it demands nothing difficult of the people inside it.

Researcher Brené Brown named this dynamic common enemy intimacy: the bond that forms when people connect not through shared values but through shared opposition.[1]

You've felt it. A sarcastic comment about a public figure lands in a room and suddenly everyone relaxes. An eye roll about a policy becomes a moment of recognition. A mutual frustration about a group you both distrust creates the sensation of being understood.

The connection feels real. It signals alignment. It says: we see things the same way, we're on the same side, we belong together.

Brown's concern about common enemy intimacy isn't that it's dishonest. It's that it's shallow. The bond is real in the moment. What it lacks is foundation.

Two people who've connected through shared contempt know what they're against. They may know very little about what the other person values, believes, or is trying to protect. The glue is opposition which is a more fragile adhesive than most people recognize until it's tested.

That's the version of common enemy intimacy most people understand once it's named. There's a second version that the concept doesn't often examine, one that runs in the opposite direction, and it's more interesting.

What Solidarity Does to the People Inside It

The reason common enemy intimacy is so durable as a social concept is that it delivers genuine psychological rewards. It reduces loneliness immediately. It clarifies identity quickly.

It transforms the discomfort of ambiguity, the uncertainty of not knowing where you stand with someone, into the relief of shared recognition.

Social psychologists have observed for decades that groups become more cohesive when they face a shared external threat. The threat sharpens boundaries. It creates urgency. Urgency generates intensity. Intensity, as established earlier, is routinely mistaken for depth.[2]

The feeling of being pulled together against something real is nearly indistinguishable, from the inside, from the feeling of genuine connection built through time and mutual understanding.

The long term cost of building connection this way is that the bond requires the enemy to remain present. If the threat disappears, the connection weakens. If someone inside the group softens their opposition, the group may experience that softening as betrayal. The shallow connection that felt like solidarity becomes a mechanism for policing loyalty. Nuance becomes inconvenient. Complexity becomes a threat to the bond itself.[3]

Sustained opposition also narrows perception over time. The opposing group stops being a collection of individuals with mixed motives and complicated beliefs. It becomes a caricature. The stories that confirm their worst qualities become memorable. The stories that humanize them become easy to dismiss. Empathy, which requires seeing the other person as a full human being, quietly erodes.[4]

This is the standard account of common enemy intimacy. It's accurate. It's also incomplete.

The Direction Nobody Expects

Alex Pretti was thirty-seven years old and worked as a nurse at a Veterans Affairs hospital in Minneapolis.[5] He spent his days caring for the people the federal government sent to war. He carried a legal firearm to a protest on January 24, 2026, and was killed by the federal government he served.[6]

Pretti had a valid carry permit. Bystander videos verified by Reuters, the BBC, the Wall Street Journal, and the Associated Press showed him holding his phone, not his weapon, as agents wrestled him to the ground.[7]

He was shot multiple times after being disarmed.[8]

The administration's response was immediate and followed a predictable pattern. U.S. Attorney Bill Essayli posted publicly that approaching law enforcement with a gun meant you were "highly likely" to be legally shot.[9] FBI Director Kash Patel said you cannot bring a loaded firearm to a protest.[10] Homeland Security Secretary Kristi Noem accused Pretti of brandishing his weapon and attacking agents.[11] Trump himself said, plainly: "You can't walk in with guns. You just can't."[12]

What happened next was not part of the expected script.

The National Rifle Association called Essayli's comments "dangerous and wrong" and demanded a full investigation.[13] Gun Owners of America stated directly that carrying a firearm at a protest is a constitutionally protected right, one that federal agents cannot use as justification for lethal force.[14] The Minnesota Gun Owners Caucus said the same.[15]

Republican Congressman Thomas Massie said carrying a firearm is not a death sentence and that anyone who believes otherwise has no business in law enforcement.[16] The NRA's rebuke was particularly notable: the organization called for responsible public voices to await a full investigation rather than making generalizations and demonizing law abiding citizens.[17]

The people issuing these statements were not immigration reform advocates. They were not critics of the administration's broader agenda. Many had been consistent supporters of the president and his policies.

What they shared with protesters, immigration activists, and civil liberties groups in that moment was not ideology. It was a principle: the Second Amendment protects the right to bear arms, including at a protest, and a government that kills a legally armed citizen and then argues the weapon justified the killing has violated something fundamental.

Common enemy intimacy had run in reverse. The shared adversary was not an opposing political group. It was a specific claim, made by a specific administration, that Second Amendment rights disappear when a law enforcement agent decides they're inconvenient.

What Makes the Reversal Possible

The standard operation of common enemy intimacy bonds people who already agree. It confirms existing alignments and sharpens existing divisions. The NRA and immigration activists finding themselves on the same side is not the standard operation.

What allowed it was a specific feature of the moment: the administration's argument threatened something that the gun rights community had spent decades treating as non-negotiable. The Second Amendment, in their framework, protects the right of citizens to be armed against government overreach. A government agent killing an armed citizen and then arguing the gun made the killing justified was precisely the scenario that framework existed to address.

The threat landed on a principle rather than an identity. The gun rights groups weren't agreeing with the protesters about immigration enforcement or about the administration's broader agenda. They were upholding a constitutional principle that happened, in this instance, to mean standing behind someone they would not ordinarily have stood behind.

This is the condition that makes reverse common enemy intimacy possible: when an action by a shared adversary violates a principle that two historically opposed groups both hold, opposition to that action doesn't require agreement about anything else. The bridge is narrow. It may not last. While it exists, though, it creates a moment of genuine shared ground where none existed before.

Psychologist Jonathan Haidt's research on moral foundations, introduced in an earlier chapter, names what happened.[18] His framework identifies care, fairness, loyalty, authority, and sanctity as the foundations people draw on when making moral judgments. What the Pretti case created was a convergence on fairness and liberty. The shared judgment was this: a government that exercises lethal force and then cites the victim's constitutional rights to justify it has crossed a line that loyalty to any faction cannot excuse. When the violation is clear enough, loyalty to a faction becomes less important than loyalty to the principle.

That shift doesn't happen often. When it does, it creates an opening that wouldn't otherwise exist.

The durability of that bridge depends on what the groups do with it. If they treat the shared principle as evidence that the other group is, in some broader sense, correct, they're likely to be disappointed. The NRA's defense of Pretti's Second Amendment rights didn't mean the NRA had changed its position on immigration enforcement. Immigration activists' recognition of the NRA's statement didn't mean they'd become gun rights advocates. The overlap was specific, not general. Treating it as general is how the moment gets wasted.

Treating the overlap as entirely meaningless wastes it too. A moment in which two groups discover they share a principle, even a single one, even in a specific context, is a moment in which both groups have demonstrated to each other that the other side is not entirely alien. That's not nothing. It's often the only crack through which a different kind of conversation can begin.

What to Do With the Opening

The mistake most people make with moments like the one the Pretti case created is treating them as either more significant than they are or less.

The more significant error assumes that because two groups agreed on this principle, they're capable of a broader alignment. They may not be. The NRA's rebuttal of the administration's framing of Pretti's death didn't indicate a shift in the organization's position on immigration enforcement, on the administration itself, or on any of the dozens of other issues that divide it from the groups who were protesting in Minneapolis.

Treating the moment as a political conversion rather than a specific convergence usually results in the moment collapsing under the weight of expectations it was never built to carry.

The less significant error assumes that because the convergence was narrow, it was meaningless. That error is costlier. Narrow convergences are the only kind of convergence available to groups that have been deeply opposed.

You can't begin with agreement on everything. You can only begin with agreement on something. The question is whether both sides are willing to let that specific agreement exist without immediately using it to revive every other disagreement.

The practical use of a reverse common enemy intimacy moment is not ideological. It's relational. It creates a brief period in which two groups have demonstrated to each other that they share at least one principle.

That shared principle doesn't build trust by itself. However, it creates the precondition for trust. The recognition that the other side is not entirely defined by the qualities that made them adversarial.

Think about a group you've spent years treating as the opposition, not as individuals you disagree with on specific questions, but as a category you've learned to read as wrong about most things, motivated by bad values, and not worth engaging seriously.

Now imagine that group publicly defending a principle you hold, not performing it, not adopting it strategically, but genuinely staking their credibility on it in a moment when doing so cost them something. The discomfort that produces is not pleasant.

It requires you to hold two things at once: your disagreement with most of what they stand for, and the evidence that they're capable of standing for something you'd stand for too.

Most people resolve that discomfort quickly. They find a reason the defense was cynical, or incomplete, or motivated by self-interest rather than principle.[19] That resolution is the standard operation of common enemy intimacy protecting its own coherence.

That's the ground Carla reached with her brother. What the Pretti case created was the same kind of opening at a larger scale, between groups with longer histories of opposition.

The Limit of the Mechanism

Common enemy intimacy, even in its bridging form, has a ceiling.

The bond it creates is reactive. It forms in response to something, not in the construction of something. Two groups that have discovered a shared adversary have not necessarily discovered a shared vision.

They've discovered a shared resistance. That resistance can hold them together long enough to accomplish something specific, but it doesn't automatically generate the mutual understanding, the recognition of each other's underlying values, or the trust required for durable cooperation.

The movements that have used shared opposition most effectively understand this distinction.

Opposition mobilizes.

Values sustain.

Groups that begin with a shared adversary and never develop a shared affirmative vision often find that when the adversary is defeated or diminished, the bond dissolves. The solidarity that felt powerful turns out to have been dependent on the threat that generated it.[20]

The Pretti case created a genuine moment. Whether anything was built from it depended on whether the groups involved recognized the moment for what it was. It was not a sign that they agreed about everything, not evidence that the other side had converted, but a single point of genuine shared ground from which a conversation could begin.

That kind of beginning is rare.

It's also fragile.

It requires both sides to resist the pull toward the standard operation of common enemy intimacy, the pull toward using the shared opposition to reinforce existing group identities rather than to examine what the principle underneath it might actually mean for how they engage with each other.

What the NRA and the immigration activists had, briefly, was a view of each other that neither had sought. Each saw the other defend something that group genuinely valued.

That's not agreement.

It's not alliance.

It's something smaller and more durable than either. It's the knowledge that the person you've been treating as the enemy is capable of standing on the same ground you're standing on. That knowledge doesn't resolve anything. It does makes resolution possible in a way that contempt never could.

What comes next examines how the systems people live inside shape which beliefs feel available to hold, and why some ideas feel thinkable in certain environments and not in others.

Chapter Summary

- Common enemy intimacy is the bond that forms when people connect through shared opposition rather than shared values. It delivers belonging quickly and feels like depth because intensity is easily mistaken for depth.
- The mechanism is reliable as a tool for building group cohesion. It also carries predictable long-term costs: the bond requires continued opposition to survive, nuance becomes inconvenient, and

the opposing group gradually loses its humanity as caricature replaces complexity.

- The same mechanism can run in reverse. When an action by a shared adversary violates a principle that two historically opposed groups both hold, opposition to that action can create a bridge where none existed. The Pretti case demonstrated this: a government's argument that a legally armed citizen's weapon justified killing him united the NRA and immigration activists around a constitutional principle neither group was willing to abandon.

- The bridging form of common enemy intimacy requires a specific condition: the shared adversary must be threatening a principle rather than an identity. Opposition to specific actions can coexist with disagreement about most everything else. Opposition to categories of people cannot.

- Narrow convergences are the only convergences available to groups with long histories of opposition. Treating a specific point of agreement as evidence of broad alignment usually collapses the moment. Treating it as meaningless wastes the only opening available.

- The bond created by shared opposition is reactive, not constructive. Opposition mobilizes. Values sustain. Groups that never develop a shared affirmative vision beyond the shared adversary often find the bond dissolves when the threat recedes.

- The opening that a reverse common enemy intimacy moment creates is not ideological. It's relational. It allows two groups to discover that the other side is not entirely defined by what makes them adversarial. That recognition is not agreement. It's the precondition for a different kind of conversation.

Chapter 12

What a Society Does With What It Knows

The Walk That Shouldn't Have Been Necessary

Nineteen Buddhist monks in saffron and maroon robes walked out of the Huong Dao Vipassana Bhavana Center in Fort Worth, Texas, on October 26, 2025, and turned east.

They were heading to Washington, D.C. The route they planned covered 2,300 miles through Louisiana, Mississippi, Alabama, Georgia, the Carolinas, and Virginia. Three of the monks chose to walk barefoot or in thin socks, to feel the ground directly and stay present in each step.

They carried no demands.

They issued no political platform.

The stated purpose of the Walk for Peace was to advocate for peace through presence, mindful steps, and open hearts. They brought a rescue dog named Aloka, whose name means "divine light" in Sanskrit, and who had walked beside the head monk, Venerable Bhikkhu Pannakara, on a previous pilgrimage across India years before.[1]

They walked more than twenty miles a day. They held a peace sharing talk at every lunch stop, weather permitting, and another at their night rest. They handed out small peace bracelets to people they met along the route.

A truck struck their escort vehicle outside Houston that November. Two monks were injured. Venerable Maha Dam Phommasan, the abbot of a temple in Georgia, had his lower leg amputated. He recovered, rejoined the group near Washington, and entered the final arena in a wheelchair.[2]

Aloka also had surgery in January for a ligament injury. He was back on the road quickly with expert veterinary care.[3]

They arrived at the Chain Bridge between Virginia and Washington at seven in the morning on February 10, 2026, after 108 days. Thousands of people lined the icy sidewalks to watch them cross. Nearly 3,500 packed American University's Bender Arena in silence as the monks walked in, offering no cheering, only quiet, as a sign of respect.

Over 20,000 people watched the livestream simultaneously, logging in from Jamaica, Germany,

Sri Lanka, and Thailand.[4] The monks stopped at Washington National Cathedral that afternoon, where more than 100 other monks and nuns from across Buddhist traditions joined them, alongside interfaith leaders including Episcopal Bishop Mariann Budde. The following day they walked to the Lincoln Memorial for the concluding ceremony.[5]

By the time they arrived, the Walk for Peace Facebook page had reached 2.9 million followers. Their Instagram had 1.9 million.[6]

What the Monks Were Not Doing

Dr. Long Si Dong, a spokesperson for the temple, was specific about what the Walk for Peace was not. It was not a political movement. It was not focused on advocacy or legislation. It was, in his words, a spiritual offering, an invitation to live peace through everyday actions, mindful steps, and open hearts.[7]

That clarity matters because of what it reveals about why the walk resonated the way it did.

The monks weren't offering a solution to American political division. They weren't claiming one side was right or another was wrong. They weren't marching against anything. What they were offering was a demonstration, sustained across 108 days and 2,300 miles, that a different quality of presence was possible.

They walked quietly through a country that had spent years saturating itself with noise. They stopped each day to share what they'd learned about peace. They handed people bracelets. They let Aloka walk beside them. When critics appeared in the comment sections of their livestreams, viewers responded by wishing that person peace. The monks themselves did the same.

The country they were walking through was not at peace. The city they were walking toward was, in early 2026, at the center of a level of political conflict that had become the defining image of American life to observers abroad. The monks understood this. They weren't denying it.

The temple's spokesperson described their belief that when peace is cultivated within, it naturally ripples outward into society.[7] That's a different claim from any political argument. It's a claim about sequence: the inner precedes the outer, and you can't force the outer to change by bypassing the inner.

What Aloka Was Actually Doing

Over those 108 days, Aloka became one of the more followed figures in the walk's social media presence. That fact is easy to dismiss as a curiosity and easy to misread as sentiment. Neither response gets at what was actually happening.

A dog doesn't carry ideology.

Aloka walked beside the monks through Alabama, through Georgia, through the Carolinas, through the cold of a Virginia February, and he did so without a position on any of the questions tearing the country apart. People who encountered the walk along the route responded to him the way people respond to animals in tense environments: defenses dropped.

The monks understood this. Pannakara had walked with Aloka before. The dog's presence wasn't incidental. It was part of the quality of presence the walk was trying to embody.

Researchers who study what lowers emotional temperature in polarized conversations point consistently to the same mechanism: before reasoning can happen, the threat signal has to reduce. When threat perception is high, the mind stops evaluating and starts defending.[8]

The monks' entire approach was designed to reduce the threat signal: the robes, the silence, the barefoot walking, the peace bracelets, the dog. None of these things addressed a policy. All of them addressed the emotional precondition that makes any conversation about policy possible.

When Aloka had his surgery in January and rejoined the walk within days,[3] the response from the walk's millions of followers was striking.

People who had been watching an act of spiritual discipline through the American South found themselves relieved that a dog was going to be alright.

That relief was real.

In a country where finding common ground had become structurally difficult, it was also a moment of genuine shared feeling that had nothing to do with who anyone voted for.

That's not trivial. Shared feeling is where common ground has to start from before it can become anything else.

The Mechanism at the Scale of Society

The psychological mechanisms described across these pages operate on individuals. Individuals are embedded in social systems, though, and social systems create the conditions under which those mechanisms either intensify or weaken.

Anchoring and priming, described earlier, determine which ideas feel available to consider before any conscious evaluation begins.[9]

A society saturated with images of irreconcilable division primes its members to expect irreconcilable division, which makes them interpret ambiguous interactions as hostile, which produces actual hostility. That generates more images of irreconcilable division. The cycle sustains itself because the information environment rewards the content that keeps it going.

Common enemy intimacy, described in an earlier chapter, bonds people through shared opposition rather than shared values.[10] A media environment optimized for engagement is, structurally, an environment optimized for common enemy intimacy.

Outrage travels because it identifies an enemy and invites the reader to join the group opposing it.[11] Every platform that profits from engagement is, in that sense, a machine for producing shared opposition at scale, whether or not anyone designed it to function that way.

What makes this problem genuinely difficult at the societal level is the same thing that made it difficult at the individual level: the mechanisms don't feel like mechanisms from inside them.

Division feels like accurate perception of a divided world.

Contempt feels like a reasonable response to contemptible behavior.

The news feed that selects for outrage feels like a window onto what's actually happening, not a curated exhibition of the most extreme expression of what's happening. A society running these mechanisms at full speed looks, from inside it, like a society that is simply being honest about how bad things are.

The question isn't whether things are bad. The question is what the evidence is actually showing, who selected it, and what the selection process leaves out.

What Gets Counted and What Doesn't

Conflict travels. Cooperation doesn't.

An argument that escalates generates engagement at every stage: the provocation, the response, the counterresponse, the commentary on the commentary. An argument that doesn't escalate, that stays at the level of two people working through a genuine disagreement and arriving somewhere unexpected, generates almost nothing.

It doesn't trend.

It doesn't get shared.

It produces no screenshots, no outrage cycles. It simply happens, invisibly, in the ordinary environments where most of human life actually takes place.[11]

The result is a systematic distortion of what people believe is representative.

The content reaching the largest audiences was produced by the most extreme expression of any disagreement.

The content representing most people's actual daily experience, the functional cooperation across differences that holds workplaces and neighborhoods and families together, is not content at all. It has no format. It generates no signal.

Peaceful Protest and the Evidence It Creates

The problem isn't scale. It's visibility. Most people can't see the people already practicing what this book has described because those people aren't doing it publicly, they aren't getting attention for doing it, and aren't being counted by any of the systems tracking what's happening in the culture.

Political scientists Erica Chenoweth and Maria Stephan spent years studying exactly this question. They built a dataset spanning hundreds of movements across decades and continents. Their central finding found that the fraction of a population required to shift a society's direction is consistently smaller than most people assume. The work isn't recruiting a majority. It's making the existing fraction visible enough to be counted.[12]

The Walk for Peace arrived in Washington while another kind of civic gathering had been building across the country for months. It was louder, more explicitly political, and making a different kind of argument. Both were peaceful. Both were doing something the information environment was structurally designed to suppress.

Throughout 2025, millions of Americans participated in demonstrations under the banner of the No Kings movement. Erica Chenoweth's Crowd Counting Consortium, which has been tracking protest data in the United States since 2017, found that by mid-2025 the number of protest events was running at more than three times the rate of the equivalent period in any prior year.[13]

More notable than the volume was the character of what was happening: Chenoweth's data showed that over 99.5 percent of those thousands of protests featured no injuries, no arrests, and no property damage.[14]

The June 2025 demonstrations drew an estimated five million people across more than 2,000 cities and towns. The October protests drew nearly seven million across approximately 2,700 locations, a record for protest participation in a single day in American history. Not one participant was arrested.[15]

That record matters not only as a civic achievement but as a counter to a specific tactic with a long history. Governments across many contexts and many eras have characterized peaceful opposition movements as violent threats to public order.

The tactic works through the same mechanism this book has described throughout: it constructs a narrative designed to produce a specific emotional response, circulates it through channels with institutional authority, and relies on the audience not having access to contradictory evidence.

The Bridging Divides Initiative at Princeton, which tracked protest data across 2025, found that violent or contentious activity occurred at just 0.5 percent of all demonstrations that year. The gap between the characterization and the documented reality was not ambiguous. It was measurable and large.[16]

Peaceful protest is one of the oldest tools available to a society trying to close that gap. When a movement documents itself behaving with discipline and restraint across thousands of events while being described publicly as dangerous, it's doing something more than exercising a constitutional right.

It's producing evidence that travels, evidence the official narrative has to account for or abandon. The nonviolence isn't only a moral choice. It's a specific, structured plan for how to establish evidence of nonviolence.

Chenoweth's historical research, drawn from that global dataset spanning more than a century of movements, identified a threshold: no government has successfully resisted a challenge when 3.5 percent of the population has mobilized in sustained peaceful protest.

That figure represents approximately 12 million Americans. The October 2025 demonstrations reached roughly two percent. The significance isn't that the threshold wasn't crossed. The significance is that a movement publicly characterized as dangerous and fringe had reached that scale while remaining, by every measurable indicator, peaceful.

When the characterization and the reality separate completely enough for the gap to become visible, the characterization loses its power to prime the people who haven't yet formed a view.[12]

What Nonviolence Actually Demonstrates

The Walk for Peace's refusal to mirror the hostility visible in the culture around it was not naivety. It was method. The No Kings protests' insistence on documented nonviolence while official voices described them as threatening was not passivity. It was also method, and both were different expressions of the same underlying logic.

The method shapes what the movement can become. A movement built on contempt for the people it opposes can produce policy changes. It can rarely produce the kind of social shift that makes those changes durable, because the people it condemned are still present, still organized, and now more unified by grievance than they were before.

Chenoweth and Stephan found that nonviolent movements succeeded at significantly higher rates partly because they reduced exactly that backlash, and partly because they drew broader participation, reaching into communities that didn't already agree.

When a movement's geographic reach extends to people who weren't already sympathetic, it's become harder to caricature as fringe.[12]

A movement that documents itself behaving with discipline and restraint, especially while being publicly described as threatening, builds a different kind of record. That record is the argument: not the speeches, not the signs, but the behavior sustained over time, at scale, across thousands of events in thousands of communities.

The monks had been practicing that for 108 days before they arrived in Washington. The protesters had been practicing it for months. Neither group was doing the same thing. Both were building the same kind of evidence.

Harder to Use

A society is not a single mind. It is made of minds, though, and the patterns those minds run, individually and collectively, determine what the society is capable of.

The knowledge this book has tried to make legible, that the mind shortcuts, anchors, protects identity, bonds through opposition, mistakes intensity for depth, and generates certainty faster than evidence warrants, is not comfortable knowledge.

It implicates everyone. It describes tendencies that operate regardless of education, regardless of political affiliation, regardless of how carefully a person believes they think.[17]

The reader who has spent eleven chapters identifying these patterns in other people's behavior is, if the book has done its job, also sitting with the recognition that those same patterns operate in their own.

That recognition is the point, not the discomfort.

The discomfort is incidental.

The point is that a person who understands these mechanisms is harder to run them on, not immune, but harder. The journalist who knew how fast thinking works still published in eleven minutes, and knowing it was what eventually made the correction possible. The family mediator still had forty minutes at Thanksgiving, and knowing the mechanism was what made the phone call three days later possible.

Knowledge doesn't prevent the mechanism from operating. It creates the gap between the mechanism operating and the conclusion being treated as final.

At the scale of a society, that gap is everything.

A population that has learned that the feeling of certainty is not the same as evidence, that the intensity of belonging is not the same as depth of understanding, that the person on the other side of a disagreement is running the same cognitive architecture, that population is harder to mobilize through contempt, harder to manipulate through outrage, harder to divide through the production of shared enemies, not impossible to reach, but harder.[17]

Harder, compounded across millions of individual decisions over years, is how social climates actually shift.

The Question the Book Ends With

This book opened with Colin Powell standing before the United Nations Security Council in 2003. He was presenting satellite imagery and audio recordings and detailed diagrams as evidence for a war, with total credibility and total confidence. He was almost entirely wrong because the instrument he was using to navigate, the human mind operating inside a system that controlled what information reached it, had been given false readings and did what minds do: it made them feel like clarity.[18]

This book has spent eleven chapters describing the ways that instrument, the human mind navigating a complex information environment, generates false certainty, protects identity at the cost of accuracy, mistakes familiarity for truth, and bonds through opposition when it could bond through understanding.

The question this book ends with is the same question it opened with: now that you know how the instrument works, what do you do with that knowledge?

The answer isn't simple and this book won't pretend it is. Knowing how motivated reasoning works doesn't stop motivated reasoning. Knowing how common enemy intimacy operates doesn't make you immune to the warmth of a group that agrees about who's wrong. Knowing how fast thinking dresses itself as accuracy doesn't stop it from arriving before you've had a chance to slow it down.

What the knowledge does is create a gap: a pause, a moment between the stimulus and the response where evaluation can happen. The gap is small. It's the gap Miriam used when she wrote the correction she was afraid to write. It's the gap Owen learned to insert between a claim arriving and a conclusion forming.

It's the gap Carla sat with for twenty minutes before she picked up her phone. It's the gap Pannakara was embodying on every one of those 108 days, moving through a country in conflict at a pace slow enough to feel the ground beneath his feet, and quiet enough in his presence to let the people he passed hear something other than noise.

It's the gap the protesters maintained between provocation and response across thousands of events in hundreds of cities, while being told they were dangerous.

The gap doesn't resolve anything by itself. Nothing resolves without it, though. A mind that can create it, even sometimes, even imperfectly, even in the situations where it matters most and is therefore hardest to find, is a mind the world cannot entirely use against itself.

That's not a trait. It's a practice. Every person willing to practice it is, in the precise and measurable sense that Chenoweth and Stephan's research describes, part of the fraction that changes things.[12]

Chapter Summary

- Nineteen Buddhist monks walked 2,300 miles from Fort Worth, Texas, to Washington, D.C., arriving on February 10, 2026, after 108 days. They carried no demands. The Walk for Peace drew millions of followers worldwide and thousands to silent witness on the streets of Washington.

- What it made visible wasn't a political argument. It was a quality of presence most people recognized and hadn't seen represented in their country for a long time.

- Peaceful protest is one of the oldest tools available to a society trying to close the gap between what authority claims and what is actually true. A movement that documents itself behaving with discipline across thousands of events while being publicly described as dangerous is producing evidence that travels, evidence the official narrative has to account for or abandon. The nonviolence isn't only a moral choice. It's an evidentiary strategy.

- Governments across many contexts and many eras have characterized peaceful opposition as violent threat. The tactic works through the same mechanism this book has described throughout: a narrative constructed to produce fear, circulated by authoritative sources, relying on the audience lacking access to contradictory evidence. Sustained, documented nonviolence is what makes that tactic fail. It generates the contradictory evidence.

- Conflict travels. Cooperation doesn't. The information environment most people navigate selects for the most extreme expression of any disagreement and filters out the ordinary cooperation constituting most of actual human life. The result is a curated exhibition of society's loudest edge, mistaken for the whole.

- Chenoweth and Stephan's research, drawn from hundreds of movements across more than a century, found that no government has successfully resisted a challenge when 3.5 percent of the population mobilizes in sustained peaceful protest. The fraction required isn't a majority. The problem isn't scale. It's visibility.

- Aloka walked 2,300 miles beside the monks. His presence did something no argument could: it reduced the threat signal before any reasoning was possible. That's not sentiment. It's the precondition all the reasoning depends on.

- The psychological mechanisms this book has described operate at the scale of societies as well as individuals. A mind that understands them is harder to run them on, not immune, but harder. Harder, compounded across millions of people over years, is how social climates shift.

- The gap between mechanism and conclusion is the whole practice: small, difficult, and the only place where things can go differently. A mind that can create it, even imperfectly, even in the moments when it's hardest to find, is a mind the world cannot entirely use against itself. That's not a trait. It's a practice. Every person willing to practice it is part of the fraction that changes things.

POINTS TO PONDER

ONE STATEMENT, FIVE ROOMS

Consider this:

"I believe God created Bigfoot."

Notice what happens when you read that. Your reaction is data. It tells you which set of commitments you were already carrying when those words arrived.

Five people hear the same statement, and five completely different reactions follow.

A committed believer in God says:
"Hooray! You're one of us!"

A committed believer in cryptids says:
"Hooray! You're one of us!"

A member of a native tribe says:
"You're wrong. Bigfoot was born from the mountain."

An atheist says: "To each his own."

A mental health professional says:
"We have a bed ready and waiting for you on the third floor."

The statement, the words, and the speaker were identical, yet five people might as well have heard five entirely different things.

Every mechanism the book examines, belief formation, identity protection, motivated reasoning, the full architecture of how minds protect what they hold, is about to appear in a single sentence. What does a statement actually do when it lands in a room full of different minds? What can you learn about your own mind by watching what it does to theirs?

Why The Room Splits

Each of the five responses comes from a different set of prior commitments, not a different level of intelligence, not a different degree of honesty, and not a different quality of character.

Both believers heard confirmation. The God believer and the cryptid believer received the same social signal through entirely different doors: someone new is standing on their side, on a line drawn long ago. The relief that generates is social rather than intellectual. It says: I'm not alone in this.

The content is almost irrelevant to either of them. What registers is the pattern: conviction confirmed, territory recognized, and identity reinforced. Two people, two wholly different belief systems, one identical response. That alone tells you something about what the response is really tracking.

The tribal member hears something different, not recruitment but displacement. The statement isn't a claim about whether Bigfoot exists. It's a claim about where Bigfoot came from, and that origin story already belongs to someone. The reaction isn't hostility to the belief itself; it's the resistance any community produces when an outsider claims ownership of something already spoken for.

The atheist's response is the most instructive of the five, and the easiest to misread. "To each his own" looks like the absence of a framework, but it isn't. Nobody arrives at complete indifference to both God and Bigfoot without having already closed the door on both questions somewhere earlier. The disengagement isn't neutral ground, it's the end state of a prior process, a long sequence of conclusions that left nothing in the statement worth engaging. The atheist isn't standing outside the room. He is standing in a room of his own construction.

The mental health professional applies a clinical lens to the combination. A claim that can't be tested paired with a claim that has no physical evidence behind it is exactly the kind of combination a clinical professional is trained to flag. The joke is funny, and it's also the only response of the five that doesn't keep the speaker in the room. The believers celebrated them, the tribal member contested them, the atheist tolerated them. The professional's response relocates them to a different floor entirely. That's the most powerful move in the set, and the most important one to recognize in yourself.

The Fault Lines Were Already There

Those five listeners weren't aligned before the statement arrived. The most striking evidence of that isn't the distance between the God believer and the atheist, which is obvious, but the distance between the two people who said the same thing. Both believers responded with "hooray," yet one believes in God and the other doesn't. Their identical reaction conceals a chasm. The tribal member's origin story was in tension with Western theological structures long before this sentence was spoken. The statement didn't create those fault lines, it lit them up.

This matters because divisiveness is often blamed on the statement rather than the soil it lands in. Almost every claim about belief, identity, or meaning will produce divergent reactions in a room full of people who carry different histories. The more useful question isn't whether a statement divides a room. It's whether the division was already there.

A statement that triggers strong, competing responses is often doing you a service: it makes visible the architecture of commitments that you otherwise navigate without noticing. That discomfort isn't the problem. It's the information.

Whether the statement is used divisively depends entirely on what happens next. If the speaker uses those reactions to sort people into allies and opponents, it becomes a tool. If you use them to understand something about why people who are otherwise reasonable arrive at such different conclusions, the same statement becomes something more valuable.

The Biases In The Room

Every person in this scenario carries assumptions about the statement. You do too. The assumptions most worth naming are the ones you're most likely to have brought with you.

The tribal member may bring a prior belief that Western structures, whether religious or scientific, tend to colonize indigenous knowledge systems rather than engage them. The statement doesn't arrive neutrally, it carries a long history of other people's explanations displacing the ones that were already there.

The atheist's tolerance may carry its own quiet condescension. "To each his own" is a generous posture. It can also be the response of someone who has already decided the conversation isn't worth having.

The mental health professional's joke deserves the most scrutiny. It works because it treats an unusual combination of beliefs as a symptom rather than a position worth engaging. It removes the speaker from the company of people whose claims merit serious attention and places them among those who simply need care. Sometimes that's appropriate. When used reflexively against any belief outside the professional's own structure, it's a way of winning an argument without having it.

Now consider your own reaction to the statement. If you found it funny, notice whether the humor came from genuine absurdity or from the comfortable distance of already knowing the answer. If you felt mild sympathy for the speaker, notice whether that sympathy extended to engaging the claim or stopped at tolerating it. If your first instinct was clinical, notice what that instinct protected you from having to take seriously. The most consequential bias in the room isn't any of the five named above. It's the one you brought with you and haven't named yet.

What This Book Has Been Explaining

The twelve chapters of this book explained that the way people process information is shaped by forces operating mostly below the level of conscious deliberation. Those forces aren't abstract. They're visible in each of the five people standing in this room, and you'll find them in yourself.

The two believers who said "hooray" are demonstrating the illusory truth effect and identity attachment working together. The statement felt true to them not because they evaluated it carefully but because it confirmed what they already believed and signaled membership in a community that shares it. Repetition and social reinforcement do the same work in less dramatic settings every day.

The tribal member's resistance is identity protection operating at its most coherent level. The origin story isn't just a belief to be accepted or rejected; it's structural. Challenging it challenges the group that holds it. Communities maintain coherence by treating certain stories as fixed, and that's the same mechanism that makes any belief so difficult to revise once someone has built their identity around it.

The atheist's tolerance is the bias blind spot at its most comfortable. Someone who believes they've stepped outside all structures doesn't notice the one they're standing in. Disengagement feels like neutrality, however, it rarely is.

The mental health professional's joke is motivated reasoning wearing a white coat. Reaching for diagnosis reflexively, before genuinely evaluating the claim, is the same move every other person in the room is making. The professional just has a more credentialed version of the shortcut.

None of them are villains. All of them are doing what the book described, and all of them, including YOU, are doing it constantly.

CHAPTER REFERENCE NOTES

Introduction Reference Notes

1 Burns, S. (2011). The Central Park Five: A chronicle of a city wilding. Knopf. The full account of the arrests, interrogations conducted without parents present, and the videotaped confessions is documented in chapters two through four.

2 Burns (2011). The forensic record, including the unmatched semen sample and the absence of physical evidence linking the five boys to the crime, is documented in chapter three. See also: Kassin, S. M. (2012). Why confessions trump innocence. American Psychologist, 67(6), 431–445. https://doi.org/10.1037/a0028212

3 Burns (2011); Eligon, J. (2014, June 19). New York settles with Central Park Five for $41 million. The New York Times. https://www.nytimes.com/2014/06/19/nyregion/new-york-settles-with-central-park-five-for-41-million.html

4 The anchoring heuristic was first identified in: Tversky, A., & Kahneman, D. (1974). Judgment under uncertainty: Heuristics and biases. Science, 185(4157), 1124–1131. https://doi.org/10.1126/science.185.4157.1124. For its application to everyday reasoning, see: Kahneman, D. (2011). Thinking, fast and slow. Farrar, Straus and Giroux.

5 Stanovich, K. E., & West, R. F. (2008). On the relative independence of thinking biases and cognitive ability. Journal of Personality and Social Psychology, 94(4), 672–695. https://doi.org/10.1037/0022-3514.94.4.672; Kahan, D. M., Peters, E., Dawson, E., & Slovic, P. (2017). Motivated numeracy and enlightened self-government. Behavioural Public Policy, 1(1), 54–86. https://doi.org/10.1017/bpp.2016.2

6 Hasher, L., Goldstein, D., & Toppino, T. (1977). Frequency and the conference of referential validity. Journal of Verbal Learning and Verbal Behavior, 16(1), 107–112. https://doi.org/10.1016/S0022-5371(77)80012-1; Pennycook, G., Cannon, T. D., & Rand, D. G. (2018). Prior exposure increases perceived accuracy of fake news. Journal of Experimental Psychology: General, 147(12), 1865–1880. https://doi.org/10.1037/xge0000465

7 Burton, R. A. (2008). On being certain: Believing you are right even when you're not. St. Martin's Press; Kahneman (2011).

8 Pronin, E., Lin, D. Y., & Ross, L. (2002). The bias blind spot: Perceptions of bias in self versus others. Personality and Social Psychology Bulletin, 28(3), 369–381. https://doi.org/10.1177/0146167202286008

Chapter 1 Reference Notes

1 Powell's presentation: Powell, C. (2003, February 5). U.S. Secretary of State addresses the U.N. Security Council [Transcript]. George W. Bush White House Archives. https://georgewbush-whitehouse.archives.gov/news/releases/2003/02/20030205-1.html

2 Powell's acknowledgment: Powell, C. (2005, September 8). Interview with Barbara Walters [Television broadcast]. ABC News. Reported in: CBS News. (2005, September 9). Powell calls U.N. speech "painful." https://www.cbsnews.com/news/powell-calls-un-speech-painful/

3 Powell's background and character: DeYoung, K. (2006). Soldier: The life of Colin Powell. Alfred A. Knopf.

4 Intelligence and susceptibility to bias: Stanovich, K. E. (2009). What intelligence tests miss: The psychology of rational thought. Yale University Press; Kahan, D. M. (2013). Ideology, motivated reasoning, and cognitive reflection. Judgment and Decision Making, 8(4), 407–424.

5 Motivated reasoning and neural bases: Westen, D., Blagov, P. S., Harenski, K., Kilts, C., & Hamann, S. (2006). Neural bases of motivated reasoning: An fMRI study of emotional constraints on partisan political judgment in the 2004 U.S. presidential election. Journal of Cognitive Neuroscience, 18(11), 1947–1958. https://doi.org/10.1162/jocn.2006.18.11.1947

6 Sophisticated rationalization: Taber, C. S., & Lodge, M. (2006). Motivated skepticism in the evaluation of political beliefs. American Journal of Political Science, 50(3), 755–769. https://doi.org/10.1111/j.1540-5907.2006.00214.x; Stanovich, K. E. (2011). Rationality and the reflective mind. Oxford University Press.

7 Bias blind spot: Pronin, E., Lin, D. Y., & Ross, L. (2002). The bias blind spot: Perceptions of bias in self versus others. Personality and Social Psychology Bulletin, 28(3), 369–381. https://doi.org/10.1177/0146167202286008

8 Universal mechanics of influence: Cialdini, R. B. (1984). Influence: The psychology of persuasion. William Morrow; Milgram, S. (1963). Behavioral study of obedience. Journal of Abnormal and Social Psychology, 67(4), 371–378. https://doi.org/10.1037/h0040525

9 Superiority as a barrier to reflection: Pronin, E., Lin, D. Y., & Ross, L. (2002). The bias blind spot: Perceptions of bias in self versus others. Personality and Social Psychology Bulletin, 28(3), 369–381. https://doi.org/10.1177/0146167202286008

10 Belief integration and resistance to correction: Evans, J. St. B. T., Barston, J. L., & Pollard, P. (1983). On the conflict between logic and belief in syllogistic reasoning. Memory & Cognition, 11(3), 295–306. https://doi.org/10.3758/BF03196976

11 Repetition and perceived truth: Hasher, L., Goldstein, D., & Toppino, T. (1977). Frequency and the conference of referential validity. Journal of Verbal Learning and Verbal Behavior, 16(1), 107–112. https://doi.org/10.1016/S0022-5371(77)80012-1; Dechêne, A., Stahl, C., Hansen, J., & Wänke, M. (2010). The truth about the truth: A meta-analytic review of the truth effect. Personality and Social Psychology Review, 14(2), 238–257. https://doi.org/10.1177/1088868309352251

12 Social conformity and belief adoption: Milgram, S. (1963). Behavioral study of obedience. Journal of Abnormal and Social Psychology, 67(4), 371–378. https://doi.org/10.1037/h0040525

13 Social pressure and belonging: Cialdini, R. B. (1984). Influence: The psychology of persuasion. William Morrow.

14 Expert overconfidence: Stanovich, K. E. (2009). What intelligence tests miss: The psychology of rational thought. Yale University Press; Pronin, E., & Kugler, M. B. (2007). Valuing thoughts, ignoring behavior: The introspection illusion as a source of the bias blind spot. Journal of Experimental Social Psychology, 43(4), 565–578. https://doi.org/10.1016/j.jesp.2006.05.011

15 Shame and identity defense: Tangney, J. P. (1991). Moral affect: The good, the bad, and the ugly. Journal of Personality and Social Psychology, 61(4), 598–607. https://doi.org/10.1037/0022-3514.61.4.598; Tangney, J. P., & Dearing, R. L. (2002). Shame and guilt. Guilford Press.

16 Self-affirmation and openness to information: Sherman, D. K., & Cohen, G. L. (2006). The psychology of self-defense: Self-affirmation theory. In M. P. Zanna (Ed.), Advances in experimental social psychology (Vol. 38, pp. 183–242). Academic Press. https://doi.org/10.1016/S0065-2601(06)38004-5; Miller, W. R., & Rollnick, S. (2012). Motivational interviewing: Helping people change (3rd ed.). Guilford Press.

Chapter 2 Reference Notes

1 Amsterdam false memory study: Crombag, H. F. M., Wagenaar, W. A., & van Koppen, P. J. (1996). Crashing memories and the problem of “source monitoring.” Applied Cognitive Psychology, 10(2), 95–104. https://doi.org/10.1002/(SICI)1099-0720(199604)10:2<95::AID-ACP366>3.0.CO;2-#

2 Perception as construction: Clark, A. (2013). Whatever next? Predictive brains, situated agents, and the future of cognitive science. Behavioral and Brain Sciences, 36(3), 181–204. https://doi.org/10.1017/S0140525X12000477

3 Brain as prediction machine: Clark, A. (2013). Whatever next? Predictive brains, situated agents, and the future of cognitive science. Behavioral and Brain Sciences, 36(3), 181–204. https://doi.org/10.1017/S0140525X12000477

4 Emotion shaping interpretation: Lerner, J. S., & Keltner, D. (2001). Fear, anger, and risk. Journal of Personality and Social Psychology, 81(1), 146–159. https://doi.org/10.1037/0022-3514.81.1.146; Slovic, P., Finucane, M. L., Peters, E., & MacGregor, D. G. (2002). The affect heuristic. In T. Gilovich, D. Griffin, & D. Kahneman (Eds.), Heuristics and biases: The psychology of intuitive judgment (pp. 397–420). Cambridge University Press.

5 Belief bias: Evans, J. St. B. T., Barston, J. L., & Pollard, P. (1983). On the conflict between logic and belief in syllogistic reasoning. Memory & Cognition, 11(3), 295–306. https://doi.org/10.3758/BF03196976

6 Motivated skepticism and asymmetric scrutiny: Taber, C. S., & Lodge, M. (2006). Motivated skepticism in the evaluation of political beliefs. American Journal of Political Science, 50(3), 755–769. https://doi.org/10.1111/j.1540-5907.2006.00214.x; Kunda, Z. (1990). The case for motivated reasoning. Psychological Bulletin, 108(3), 480–498. https://doi.org/10.1037/0033-2909.108.3.480

7 Evidence colliding with identity: Kunda, Z. (1990). The case for motivated reasoning. Psychological Bulletin, 108(3), 480–498. https://doi.org/10.1037/0033-2909.108.3.480

8 Social cost of belief change: Tajfel, H., & Turner, J. C. (1979). An integrative theory of intergroup conflict. In W. G. Austin & S. Worchel (Eds.), The social psychology of intergroup relations (pp. 33–47). Brooks/Cole; Sherman, D. K., & Cohen, G. L. (2006). The psychology of self-defense: Self-affirmation theory. In M. P. Zanna (Ed.), Advances in experimental social psychology (Vol. 38, pp. 183–242). Academic Press. https://doi.org/10.1016/S0065-2601(06)38004-5

9 Neurological reward for confirmation: Westen, D., Blagov, P. S., Harenski, K., Kilts, C., & Hamann, S. (2006). Neural bases of motivated reasoning: An fMRI study of emotional constraints on partisan political judgment in the 2004 U.S. presidential election. Journal of

Cognitive Neuroscience, 18(11), 1947–1958. https://doi.org/10.1162/jocn.2006.18.11.1947

10 Group membership raising cost of belief change: Tajfel, H., & Turner, J. C. (1979). An integrative theory of intergroup conflict. In W. G. Austin & S. Worchel (Eds.), The social psychology of intergroup relations (pp. 33–47). Brooks/Cole; Petty, R. E., & Cacioppo, J. T. (1986). Communication and persuasion: Central and peripheral routes to attitude change. Springer-Verlag.

11 Narrative as perceptual prior: Clark, A. (2013). Whatever next? Predictive brains, situated agents, and the future of cognitive science. Behavioral and Brain Sciences, 36(3), 181–204. https://doi.org/10.1017/S0140525X12000477; Kahneman, D. (2011). Thinking, fast and slow. Farrar, Straus and Giroux.

12 Mutual bias blind spot: Pronin, E., Lin, D. Y., & Ross, L. (2002). The bias blind spot: Perceptions of bias in self versus others. Personality and Social Psychology Bulletin, 28(3), 369–381. https://doi.org/10.1177/0146167202286008; Linville, P. W., & Jones, E. E. (1980). Polarized appraisals of out-group members. Journal of Personality and Social Psychology, 38(5), 689–703. https://doi.org/10.1037/0022-3514.38.5.689

13 Forward reference to Chapter 3 on repetition and illusory truth: see Hasher, L., Goldstein, D., & Toppino, T. (1977). Frequency and the conference of referential validity. Journal of Verbal Learning and Verbal Behavior, 16(1), 107–112. https://doi.org/10.1016/S0022-5371(77)80012-1

Chapter 3 Reference Notes

1 Illusory truth effect and persistence of repeated claims: Hasher, L., Goldstein, D., & Toppino, T. (1977). Frequency and the conference of referential validity. Journal of Verbal Learning and Verbal Behavior, 16(1), 107–112. https://doi.org/10.1016/S0022-5371(77)80012-1; Dechêne, A., Stahl, C., Hansen, J., & Wänke, M. (2010). The truth about the truth: A meta-analytic review of the truth effect. Personality and Social Psychology Review, 14(2), 238–257. https://doi.org/10.1177/1088868309352251

2 Processing fluency: Reber, R., & Schwarz, N. (1999). Effects of perceptual fluency on judgments of truth. Consciousness and Cognition, 8(3), 338–342. https://doi.org/10.1006/ccog.1999.0386; Hasher, L., Goldstein, D., & Toppino, T. (1977). Frequency and the conference of

referential validity. Journal of Verbal Learning and Verbal Behavior, 16(1), 107–112. https://doi.org/10.1016/S0022-5371(77)80012-1

3 Repetition increases perceived truth even for known falsehoods: Fazio, L. K., Brashier, N. M., Payne, B. K., & Marsh, E. J. (2015). Knowledge does not protect against illusory truth. Journal of Experimental Psychology: General, 144(5), 993–1002. https://doi.org/10.1037/xge0000098; Fazio, L. K. (2020). Repetition increases perceived truth even for known falsehoods. Collabra: Psychology, 6(1), Article 38. https://doi.org/10.1525/collabra.347

4 Prior exposure across platforms increases perceived accuracy: Pennycook, G., Cannon, T. D., & Rand, D. G. (2018). Prior exposure increases perceived accuracy of fake news. Journal of Experimental Psychology: General, 147(12), 1865–1880. https://doi.org/10.1037/xge0000465

5 Short content travels further than careful explanations: Vosoughi, S., Roy, D., & Aral, S. (2018). The spread of true and false news online. Science, 359(6380), 1146–1151. https://doi.org/10.1126/science.aap9559

6 Emotional content drives sharing: Brady, W. J., Wills, J. A., Jost, J. T., Tucker, J. A., & Van Bavel, J. J. (2017). Emotion shapes the diffusion of moralized content in social networks. Proceedings of the National Academy of Sciences, 114(28), 7313–7318. https://doi.org/10.1073/pnas.1618923114

7 Misinformation spread through ordinary sharing: Vosoughi, S., Roy, D., & Aral, S. (2018). The spread of true and false news online. Science, 359(6380), 1146–1151. https://doi.org/10.1126/science.aap9559; Starbird, K., Arif, A., & Wilson, T. (2019). Disinformation as collaborative work: Surfacing the participatory nature of strategic information operations. Proceedings of the ACM on Human-Computer Interaction, 3(CSCW), Article 127. https://doi.org/10.1145/3359229

8 Social endorsement adds perceived weight: Cialdini, R. B. (1984). Influence: The psychology of persuasion. William Morrow; Vosoughi, S., Roy, D., & Aral, S. (2018). The spread of true and false news online. Science, 359(6380), 1146–1151. https://doi.org/10.1126/science.aap9559

9 Misinformation ecosystems sustained by ordinary psychology: Starbird, K., Arif, A., & Wilson, T. (2019). Disinformation as collaborative work: Surfacing the participatory nature of strategic information operations. Proceedings of the ACM on Human-Computer Interac-

tion, 3(CSCW), Article 127. https://doi.org/10.1145/3359229
10 Forward reference to Chapter 4 on belief and identity: see Tangney, J. P. (1991). Moral affect: The good, the bad, and the ugly. Journal of Personality and Social Psychology, 61(4), 598–607. https://doi.org/10.1037/0022-3514.61.4.598; Tajfel, H., & Turner, J. C. (1979). An integrative theory of intergroup conflict. In W. G. Austin & S. Worchel (Eds.), The social psychology of intergroup relations (pp. 33–47). Brooks/Cole.

Chapter 4 Reference Notes

1 Marshall's original research: Marshall, B. J., & Warren, J. R. (1984). Unidentified curved bacilli in the stomach of patients with gastritis and peptic ulceration. The Lancet, 323(8390), 1311–1315. https://doi.org/10.1016/S0140-6736(84)91816-6
2 Nobel Prize awarded to Marshall and Warren: Nobel Assembly at the Karolinska Institute. (2005). The Nobel Prize in Physiology or Medicine 2005: Barry J. Marshall and J. Robin Warren. Nobel Media AB. https://www.nobelprize.org/prizes/medicine/2005/summary/
3 Guilt vs. shame distinction: Tangney, J. P. (1991). Moral affect: The good, the bad, and the ugly. Journal of Personality and Social Psychology, 61(4), 598–607. https://doi.org/10.1037/0022-3514.61.4.598; Tangney, J. P., & Dearing, R. L. (2002).
4 Identity-linked beliefs triggering defense: Steele, C. M. (1988). The psychology of self-affirmation: Sustaining the integrity of the self. In L. Berkowitz (Ed.), Advances in experimental social psychology (Vol. 21, pp. 261–302). Academic Press; Sherman, D. K., & Cohen, G. L. (2006). The psychology of self-defense: Self-affirmation theory. In M. P. Zanna (Ed.), Advances in experimental social psychology (Vol. 38, pp. 183–242). Academic Press. https://doi.org/10.1016/S0065-2601(06)38004-5
5 Public commitment deepening identity fusion with a belief: Cialdini, R. B. (1984). Influence: The psychology of persuasion. William Morrow.
6 Social belonging shaping what feels thinkable: Tajfel, H., & Turner, J. C. (1979). An integrative theory of intergroup conflict. In W. G. Austin & S. Worchel (Eds.), The social psychology of intergroup relations (pp. 33–47). Brooks/Cole.
7 Flexible identity and openness to revision: Steele, C. M. (1988). The psychology of self-affirmation: Sustaining the integrity of the self. In L. Berkowitz (Ed.), Advances in experimental social psychology (Vol. 21,

pp. 261–302). Academic Press; Sherman, D. K., & Cohen, G. L. (2006). The psychology of self-defense: Self-affirmation theory. In M. P. Zanna (Ed.), Advances in experimental social psychology (Vol. 38, pp. 183–242). Academic Press. https://doi.org/10.1016/S0065-2601(06)38004-5

8 Motivated reasoning: Kunda, Z. (1990). The case for motivated reasoning. Psychological Bulletin, 108(3), 480–498. https://doi.org/10.1037/0033-2909.108.3.480; Taber, C. S., & Lodge, M. (2006). Motivated skepticism in the evaluation of political beliefs. American Journal of Political Science, 50(3), 755–769. https://doi.org/10.1111/j.1540-5907.2006.00214.x

9 Defensiveness felt as principled scrutiny: Pronin, E., Lin, D. Y., & Ross, L. (2002). The bias blind spot: Perceptions of bias in self versus others. Personality and Social Psychology Bulletin, 28(3), 369–381. https://doi.org/10.1177/0146167202286008

10 Public shaming hardening beliefs: Kunda, Z. (1990). The case for motivated reasoning. Psychological Bulletin, 108(3), 480–498. https://doi.org/10.1037/0033-2909.108.3.480; Tangney, J. P., & Dearing, R. L. (2002). Shame and guilt. Guilford Press.

11 Dignity-preserving approach to correction: Miller, W. R., & Rollnick, S. (2012). Motivational interviewing: Helping people change (3rd ed.). Guilford Press.

12 Mind that can revise as critical-thinking capacity: Stanovich, K. E. (2009). What intelligence tests miss: The psychology of rational thought. Yale University Press; Stanovich, K. E. (2011). Rationality and the reflective mind. Oxford University Press.

13 Forward reference to Chapter 5 on expert judgment and social architecture of belief: Tetlock, P. E. (2005). Expert political judgment: How good is it? How can we know? Princeton University Press.

Chapter 5 Reference Notes

1 Semmelweis and handwashing: Semmelweis, I. P. (1861). Die Ätiologie, der Begriff und die Prophylaxis des Kindbettfiebers. Hartleben.

2 Intelligence amplifying justification rather than catching bias: Stanovich, K. E. (2009). What intelligence tests miss: The psychology of rational thought. Yale University Press; Kahan, D. M. (2013). Ideology, motivated reasoning, and cognitive reflection. Judgment and Decision Making, 8(4), 407–424.

3 Bias blind spot: Pronin, E., Lin, D. Y., & Ross, L. (2002). The bias blind spot: Perceptions of bias in self versus others. Person-

ality and Social Psychology Bulletin, 28(3), 369–381. https://doi.org/10.1177/0146167202286008; Pronin, E., & Kugler, M. B. (2007). Valuing thoughts, ignoring behavior: The introspection illusion as a source of the bias blind spot. Journal of Experimental Social Psychology, 43(4), 565–578. https://doi.org/10.1016/j.jesp.2006.05.011

4 Motivated reasoning — asymmetric scrutiny of challenging evidence: Kunda, Z. (1990). The case for motivated reasoning. Psychological Bulletin, 108(3), 480–498. https://doi.org/10.1037/0033-2909.108.3.480; Taber, C. S., & Lodge, M. (2006). Motivated skepticism in the evaluation of political beliefs. American Journal of Political Science, 50(3), 755–769. https://doi.org/10.1111/j.1540-5907.2006.00214.x

5 Emotion as selective spotlight: Lerner, J. S., & Keltner, D. (2001). Fear, anger, and risk. Journal of Personality and Social Psychology, 81(1), 146–159. https://doi.org/10.1037/0022-3514.81.1.146; Slovic, P., Finucane, M. L., Peters, E., & MacGregor, D. G. (2002). The affect heuristic. In T. Gilovich, D. Griffin, & D. Kahneman (Eds.), Heuristics and biases: The psychology of intuitive judgment (pp. 397–420). Cambridge University Press.

6 Belief architecture and community epistemic norms: Haidt, J. (2012). The righteous mind: Why good people are divided by politics and religion. Pantheon Books; Tajfel, H., & Turner, J. C. (1979). An integrative theory of intergroup conflict. In W. G. Austin & S. Worchel (Eds.), The social psychology of intergroup relations (pp. 33–47). Brooks/Cole.

7 Expert judgment bounded by internalized framework: Tetlock, P. E. (2005). Expert political judgment: How good is it? How can we know? Princeton University Press.

8 Awareness vs. insight — knowing about bias vs. catching it in real time: Kahneman, D. (2011). Thinking, fast and slow. Farrar, Straus and Giroux.

9 Objectivity as discipline requiring deliberate friction: Klein, G. (1998). Sources of power: How people make decisions. MIT Press; Kahneman, D. (2011). Thinking, fast and slow. Farrar, Straus and Giroux.

10 Forward reference to Chapter 6 on deliberate manipulation: Cialdini, R. B. (1984). Influence: The psychology of persuasion. William Morrow; Wylie, C. (2019).

Mindf*ck: Cambridge Analytica and the plot to break America. Random House.

Chapter 6 Reference Notes

1 Cambridge Analytica psychological targeting: Wylie, C. (2019). Mindf*ck: Cambridge Analytica and the plot to break America. Random House.

2 Internal communications, whistleblower testimony, and disputed efficacy: Wylie, C. (2019). Mindf*ck: Cambridge Analytica and the plot to break America. Random House.

3 Coordinated accounts and escalation pattern: Starbird, K., Arif, A., & Wilson, T. (2019). Disinformation as collaborative work: Surfacing the participatory nature of strategic information operations. Proceedings of the ACM on Human-Computer Interaction, 3(CSCW), Article 127. https://doi.org/10.1145/3359229

4 Identity as the primary manipulation target: Tajfel, H., & Turner, J. C. (1979). An integrative theory of intergroup conflict. In W. G. Austin & S. Worchel (Eds.), The social psychology of intergroup relations (pp. 33–47). Brooks/Cole; Sherman, D. K., & Cohen, G. L. (2006). The psychology of self-defense: Self-affirmation theory. In M. P. Zanna (Ed.), Advances in experimental social psychology (Vol. 38, pp. 183–242). Academic Press. https://doi.org/10.1016/S0065-2601(06)38004-5

5 Dark Triad — Machiavellianism, narcissism, and psychopathy: Paulhus, D. L., & Williams, K. M. (2002). The Dark Triad of personality: Narcissism, Machiavellianism, and psychopathy. Journal of Research in Personality, 36(6), 556–563. https://doi.org/10.1016/S0092-6566(02)00505-6

6 Illusory truth effect deployed intentionally: Hasher, L., Goldstein, D., & Toppino, T. (1977). Frequency and the conference of referential validity. Journal of Verbal Learning and Verbal Behavior, 16(1), 107–112. https://doi.org/10.1016/S0022-5371(77)80012-1; Fazio, L. K., Brashier, N. M., Payne, B. K., & Marsh, E. J. (2015). Knowledge does not protect against illusory truth. Journal of Experimental Psychology: General, 144(5), 993–1002. https://doi.org/10.1037/xge0000098

7 Identity framing making claims personally essential: Tajfel, H., & Turner, J. C. (1979). An integrative theory of intergroup conflict. In W. G. Austin & S. Worchel (Eds.), The social psychology of intergroup relations (pp. 33–47). Brooks/Cole.

8 Emotional priming preceding belief shift: Westen, D., Blagov, P. S., Harenski, K., Kilts, C., & Hamann, S. (2006). Neural bases of motivated reasoning: An fMRI study of emotional constraints on partisan political judgment in the 2004 U.S. presidential election. Journal of

Cognitive Neuroscience, 18(11), 1947–1958. https://doi.org/10.1162/jocn.2006.18.11.1947; Lerner, J. S., & Keltner, D. (2001). Fear, anger, and risk. Journal of Personality and Social Psychology, 81(1), 146–159. https://doi.org/10.1037/0022-3514.81.1.146

9 Manufactured social proof exploiting consensus heuristic: Cialdini, R. B. (1984). Influence: The psychology of persuasion. William Morrow.

10 Personal experience as the most convincing evidence: Cialdini, R. B. (1984). Influence: The psychology of persuasion. William Morrow.

11 Propaganda as manipulation at institutional scale: Ellul, J. (1965). Propaganda: The formation of men's attitudes. Knopf.

12 Identity targeting combined with social proof bypassing evaluation: Ellul, J. (1965). Propaganda: The formation of men's attitudes. Knopf; Cialdini, R. B. (1984). Influence: The psychology of persuasion. William Morrow.

13 Self-generated conclusions more resistant to revision: Petty, R. E., & Cacioppo, J. T. (1986). Communication and persuasion: Central and peripheral routes to attitude change. Springer-Verlag.

14 Forward reference to Chapter 7 on source credibility: Cialdini, R. B. (1984). Influence: The psychology of persuasion. William Morrow; Petty, R. E., & Cacioppo, J. T. (1986). Communication and persuasion: Central and peripheral routes to attitude change. Springer-Verlag.

Chapter 7 Reference Notes

1 Challenger disaster and Rogers Commission: Presidential Commission on the Space Shuttle Challenger Accident. (1986). Report of the Presidential Commission on the Space Shuttle Challenger Accident. U.S. Government Printing Office.

2 Boisjoly's testimony and O-ring concerns: Vaughan, D. (1996). The Challenger launch decision: Risky technology, culture, and deviance at NASA. University of Chicago Press.

3 Institutional authority structure overriding engineering judgment: Vaughan, D. (1996). The Challenger launch decision: Risky technology, culture, and deviance at NASA. University of Chicago Press.

4 Authority shortcut as cognitive necessity: Cialdini, R. B. (1984). Influence: The psychology of persuasion. William Morrow.

5 Credential substituting for argument — scrutiny adjusted before content arrives: Petty, R. E., & Cacioppo, J. T. (1986). Communication and persuasion: Central and peripheral routes to attitude change. Springer-Verlag.

6 Authority heuristic operating automatically: Cialdini, R. B. (1984).

Influence: The psychology of persuasion. William Morrow; Milgram, S. (1963). Behavioral study of obedience.

Journal of Abnormal and Social Psychology, 67(4), 371–378. https://doi.org/10.1037/h0040525

7 Authority adjusting evaluation before it begins — peripheral route: Petty, R. E., & Cacioppo, J. T. (1986). Communication and persuasion: Central and peripheral routes to attitude change. Springer-Verlag.

8 Same content receiving different credibility based on source: Petty, R. E., & Cacioppo, J. T. (1986). Communication and persuasion: Central and peripheral routes to attitude change. Springer-Verlag; Cialdini, R. B. (1984). Influence: The psychology of persuasion. William Morrow.

9 Borrowed certainty — deliberate manufacture of authority signals: Wylie, C. (2019). Mindf*ck: Cambridge Analytica and the plot to break America. Random House; Ellul, J. (1965). Propaganda: The formation of men's attitudes. Knopf.

10 Domain specificity of credentials: Tetlock, P. E. (2005). Expert political judgment: How good is it? How can we know? Princeton University Press.

11 Social amplification of authority in group and institutional settings: Milgram, S. (1963). Behavioral study of obedience. Journal of Abnormal and Social Psychology, 67(4), 371–378. https://doi.org/10.1037/h0040525; Vaughan, D. (1996). The Challenger launch decision: Risky technology, culture, and deviance at NASA. University of Chicago Press.

12 Forward reference to Chapter 8 on language, framing, and perception: Clark, A. (2013). Whatever next? Predictive brains, situated agents, and the future of cognitive science. Behavioral and Brain Sciences, 36(3), 181–204. https://doi.org/10.1017/S0140525X12000477

Chapter 8 Reference Notes

1 Belief correction as identity threat: Sherman, D. K., & Cohen, G. L. (2006). The psychology of self-defense: Self-affirmation theory. In M. P. Zanna (Ed.), Advances in experimental social psychology (Vol. 38, pp. 183–242). Academic Press. https://doi.org/10.1016/S0065-2601(06)38004-5; Steele, C. M. (1988). The psychology of self-affirmation: Sustaining the integrity of the self. In L. Berkowitz (Ed.), Advances in experimental social psychology (Vol. 21, pp. 261–302). Academic Press.

2 Wrong belief as product of human cognitive tendencies, not defective thinking: Kahneman, D. (2011). Thinking, fast and slow. Farrar, Straus and Giroux.

3 Illusory truth producing settled belief without conscious deci-

sion: Hasher, L., Goldstein, D., & Toppino, T. (1977). Frequency and the conference of referential validity. Journal of Verbal Learning and Verbal Behavior, 16(1), 107–112. https://doi.org/10.1016/S0022-5371(77)80012-1; Pennycook, G., Cannon, T. D., & Rand, D. G. (2018). Prior exposure increases perceived accuracy of fake news. Journal of Experimental Psychology: General, 147(12), 1865–1880. https://doi.org/10.1037/xge0000465

4 Intelligence articulating and defending a wrong framework: Stanovich, K. E. (2009). What intelligence tests miss: The psychology of rational thought. Yale University Press; Kahan, D. M. (2013). Ideology, motivated reasoning, and cognitive reflection. Judgment and Decision Making, 8(4), 407–424.

5 Rapid reconstruction after belief collapse: Kahneman, D. (2011). Thinking, fast and slow. Farrar, Straus and Giroux; Kunda, Z. (1990). The case for motivated reasoning. Psychological Bulletin, 108(3), 480–498. https://doi.org/10.1037/0033-2909.108.3.480

6 Security in core values producing openness to challenging evidence: Steele, C. M. (1988). The psychology of self-affirmation: Sustaining the integrity of the self. In L. Berkowitz (Ed.), Advances in experimental social psychology (Vol. 21, pp. 261–302). Academic Press; Sherman, D. K., & Cohen, G. L. (2006). The psychology of self-defense: Self-affirmation theory. In M. P. Zanna (Ed.), Advances in experimental social psychology (Vol. 38, pp. 183–242). Academic Press. https://doi.org/10.1016/S0065-2601(06)38004-5

7 Process-based vs. conclusion-based confidence: Stanovich, K. E. (2009). What intelligence tests miss: The psychology of rational thought. Yale University Press; Stanovich, K. E. (2011). Rationality and the reflective mind. Oxford University Press; Klein, G. (1998). Sources of power: How people make decisions. MIT Press.

8 Healthy doubt vs. paralyzing doubt: Stanovich, K. E. (2009). What intelligence tests miss: The psychology of rational thought. Yale University Press; Tangney, J. P. (1991). Moral affect: The good, the bad, and the ugly. Journal of Personality and Social Psychology, 61(4), 598–607. https://doi.org/10.1037/0022-3514.61.4.598

9 Commitment and consistency — motivation to appear consistent with prior public statements: Cialdini, R. B. (1984). Influence: The psychology of persuasion. William Morrow.

10 Doubling down, softening without acknowledging, going silent

after public error: Cialdini, R. B. (1984). Influence: The psychology of persuasion. William Morrow; Kunda, Z. (1990). The case for motivated reasoning.

Psychological Bulletin, 108(3), 480–498. https://doi.org/10.1037/0033-2909.108.3.480

11 Provisional language and epistemic calibration: Kahneman, D. (2011). Thinking, fast and slow. Farrar, Straus and Giroux; Stanovich, K. E. (2011). Rationality and the reflective mind. Oxford University Press.

12 Integrity vs. rigidity — values-driven vs. position-driven consistency: Miller, W. R., & Rollnick, S. (2012). Motivational interviewing: Helping people change (3rd ed.). Guilford Press; Stanovich, K. E. (2009). What intelligence tests miss: The psychology of rational thought. Yale University Press.

13 Forward reference to Chapter 9 on automatic thinking: Kahneman, D. (2011). Thinking, fast and slow. Farrar, Straus and Giroux.

Chapter 9 Reference Notes

1 Kahneman's two-system framework: Kahneman, D. (2011). Thinking, fast and slow. Farrar, Straus and Giroux.

2 Fast thinking feeling identical to slow thinking from the inside: Kahneman, D. (2011). Thinking, fast and slow. Farrar, Straus and Giroux.

3 Familiarity unrelated to truth: Hasher, L., Goldstein, D., & Toppino, T. (1977). Frequency and the conference of referential validity. Journal of Verbal Learning and Verbal Behavior, 16(1), 107–112. https://doi.org/10.1016/S0022-5371(77)80012-1; Fazio, L. K., Brashier, N. M., Payne, B. K., & Marsh, E. J. (2015). Knowledge does not protect against illusory truth. Journal of Experimental Psychology: General, 144(5), 993–1002. https://doi.org/10.1037/xge0000098

4 Strong emotional states narrowing information considered: Lerner, J. S., & Keltner, D. (2001). Fear, anger, and risk. Journal of Personality and Social Psychology, 81(1), 146–159. https://doi.org/10.1037/0022-3514.81.1.146; Slovic, P., Finucane, M. L., Peters, E., & MacGregor, D. G. (2002). The affect heuristic. In T. Gilovich, D. Griffin, & D. Kahneman (Eds.), Heuristics and biases: The psychology of intuitive judgment (pp. 397–420). Cambridge University Press.

5 Relief of resolution misread as correctness: Kahneman, D. (2011). Thinking, fast and slow. Farrar, Straus and Giroux; Lerner, J. S., & Keltner, D. (2001). Fear, anger, and risk. Journal of Personality and Social Psychology, 81(1), 146–159. https://doi.org/10.1037/0022-3514.81.1.146

6 Single question as most effective friction at moment of highest confidence: Klein, G. (1998). Sources of power: How people make decisions. MIT Press.

7 Gary Klein — expert pattern recognition under pressure: Klein, G. (1998). Sources of power: How people make decisions. MIT Press.

8 Platforms amplifying emotional content: Brady, W. J., Wills, J. A., Jost, J. T., Tucker, J. A., & Van Bavel, J. J. (2017). Emotion shapes the diffusion of moralized content in social networks. Proceedings of the National Academy of Sciences, 114(28), 7313–7318. https://doi.org/10.1073/pnas.1618923114; Vosoughi, S., Roy, D., & Aral, S. (2018). The spread of true and false news online. Science, 359(6380), 1146–1151. https://doi.org/10.1126/science.aap9559

9 Repetition building false familiarity across feeds: Pennycook, G., Cannon, T. D., & Rand, D. G. (2018). Prior exposure increases perceived accuracy of fake news. Journal of Experimental Psychology: General, 147(12), 1865–1880. https://doi.org/10.1037/xge0000465

10 Language selected to close the loop before evaluation begins: Kahneman, D. (2011). Thinking, fast and slow. Farrar, Straus and Giroux; Ellul, J. (1965). Propaganda: The formation of men's attitudes. Knopf.

11 Social proof arriving before evidence is examined: Cialdini, R. B. (1984). Influence: The psychology of persuasion. William Morrow.

Chapter 10 Reference Notes

1 Motivated reasoning — Kunda named explicitly: Kunda, Z. (1990). The case for motivated reasoning. Psychological Bulletin, 108(3), 480–498. https://doi.org/10.1037/0033-2909.108.3.480; Taber, C. S., & Lodge, M. (2006). Motivated skepticism in the evaluation of political beliefs. American Journal of Political Science, 50(3), 755–769. https://doi.org/10.1111/j.1540-5907.2006.00214.x

2 Better argument producing defense rather than evaluation: Kunda, Z. (1990). The case for motivated reasoning. Psychological Bulletin, 108(3), 480–498. https://doi.org/10.1037/0033-2909.108.3.480; Westen, D., Blagov, P. S., Harenski, K., Kilts, C., & Hamann, S. (2006). Neural bases of motivated reasoning. Journal of Cognitive Neuroscience, 18(11), 1947–1958. https://doi.org/10.1162/jocn.2006.18.11.1947

3 Emotional regulation collapsing at a threshold: Lerner, J. S., & Keltner, D. (2001). Fear, anger, and risk. Journal of Personality and Social Psychology, 81(1), 146–159. https://doi.org/10.1037/0022-3514.81.1.146; Tangney, J. P., & Dearing, R. L. (2002). Shame and guilt. Guilford Press.

4 Haidt's moral foundations theory — named explicitly: Haidt, J. (2012). The righteous mind: Why good people are divided by politics and religion. Pantheon Books.

5 Shared values expressed through different threat perceptions: Graham, J., Haidt, J., & Nosek, B. A. (2009). Liberals and conservatives rely on different sets of moral foundations. Journal of Personality and Social Psychology, 96(5), 1029–1046. https://doi.org/10.1037/a0015141

6 Acknowledgment must precede challenge: Miller, W. R., & Rollnick, S. (2012). Motivational interviewing: Helping people change (3rd ed.). Guilford Press; Cialdini, R. B. (1984). Influence: The psychology of persuasion. William Morrow.

7 Genuine curiosity detectable — performed understanding fails: Miller, W. R., & Rollnick, S. (2012). Motivational interviewing: Helping people change (3rd ed.). Guilford Press.

8 Dismissing underlying concern vs. disagreeing with conclusion: Steele, C. M. (1988). The psychology of self-affirmation: Sustaining the integrity of the self. In L. Berkowitz (Ed.), Advances in experimental social psychology (Vol. 21, pp. 261–302). Academic Press; Sherman, D. K., & Cohen, G. L. (2006). The psychology of self-defense: Self-affirmation theory. In M. P. Zanna (Ed.), Advances in experimental social psychology (Vol. 38, pp. 183–242). Academic Press. https://doi.org/10.1016/S0065-2601(06)38004-5

9 Forward reference to Chapter 11 — shared opposition creating in-group bonds: Sherif, M., Harvey, O. J., White, B. J., Hood, W. R., & Sherif, C. W. (1961). Intergroup conflict and cooperation: The Robbers Cave experiment. University of Oklahoma Press; Tajfel, H., & Turner, J. C. (1979). An integrative theory of intergroup conflict. In W. G. Austin & S. Worchel (Eds.), The social psychology of intergroup relations (pp. 33–47). Brooks/Cole.

Chapter 11 Reference Notes

1 Common enemy intimacy — Brown named explicitly: Brown, B. (2017). Braving the wilderness: The quest for true belonging and the courage to stand alone. Random House.

2 Groups more cohesive under shared external threat; intensity mistaken for depth: Sherif, M., Harvey, O. J., White, B. J., Hood, W. R., & Sherif, C. W. (1961). Intergroup conflict and cooperation: The Robbers Cave experiment. University of Oklahoma Press; Tajfel, H., & Turner, J. C. (1979). An integrative theory of intergroup conflict. In W. G. Austin

& S. Worchel (Eds.), The social psychology of intergroup relations (pp. 33–47). Brooks/Cole.

3 Bond requiring enemy to remain present; policing loyalty: Tajfel, H., & Turner, J. C. (1979). An integrative theory of intergroup conflict. In W. G. Austin & S. Worchel (Eds.), The social psychology of intergroup relations (pp. 33–47). Brooks/Cole; Sherif, M., Harvey, O. J., White, B. J., Hood, W. R., & Sherif, C. W. (1961). Intergroup conflict and cooperation: The Robbers Cave experiment. University of Oklahoma Press.

4 Opposing group becoming caricature; empathy eroding: Tajfel, H., & Turner, J. C. (1979). An integrative theory of intergroup conflict. In W. G. Austin & S. Worchel (Eds.), The social psychology of intergroup relations (pp. 33–47). Brooks/Cole; Linville, P. W., & Jones, E. E. (1980). Polarized appraisals of out-group members. Journal of Personality and Social Psychology, 38(5), 689–703. https://doi.org/10.1037/0022-3514.38.5.689

5 Alex Pretti — nurse at VA hospital in Minneapolis: Lavietes, M., Melendez, P., Romero, D., & Stelloh, T. (2026, January 26). What we know about Alex Pretti, the ICU nurse killed in Minneapolis by federal officials. NBC News. https://www.nbcnews.com/news/us-news/alex-pretti-fatally-shot-federal-officers-minneapolis-identified-paren-rcna255758

6 Pretti's date of death, carry permit, and the shooting: Killing of Alex Pretti. (2026). Wikipedia. https://en.wikipedia.org/wiki/Killing_of_Alex_Pretti; CNN. (2026, January 25). January 24, 2026 — Fatal shooting of Minneapolis man. https://www.cnn.com/us/live-news/ice-minneapolis-shooting-01-24-26 [Note: The chapter's original date of January 25 has been corrected to January 24, the confirmed date of the shooting per Wikipedia and contemporaneous news reporting.]

7 Bystander videos showing Pretti holding phone, not weapon: CBS News. (2026, January 26). In Alex Pretti's killing, a sharp contrast between what Trump officials say and what video shows. CBS News. https://www.cbsnews.com/news/alex-pretti-shooting-contrast-official-accounts-videos

8 Pretti shot multiple times after being disarmed: CNN. (2026, January 27). Gun-rights groups decried the administration's rhetoric on Alex Pretti's gun. CNN Politics. https://www.cnn.com/2026/01/27/politics/gun-alex-pretti-ice-nra

9 Essayli's post: Stafford, J., & Stern, M. (2026, January 25). The

Trump administration is lying about gun rights and the death of Alex Pretti. Reason. https://reason.com/2026/01/25/the-trump-administration-is-lying-about-gun-rights-and-the-death-of-alex-pretti

10 Patel statement on firearms at protests: PBS News. (2026, January 27). Killing of Alex Pretti scrambles Second Amendment politics for Trump. PBS NewsHour. https://www.pbs.org/newshour/politics/killing-of-alex-pretti-scrambles-second-amendment-politics-for-trump

11 Noem accusation: Al Jazeera. (2026, January 25). Who was Alex Pretti, the nurse shot dead by federal agents in Minneapolis? Al Jazeera. https://www.aljazeera.com/news/2026/1/25/who-was-alex-pretti-the-nurse-shot-dead-by-federal-agents-in-minneapolis

12 Trump's statement: CNN. (2026, January 27). Gun-rights groups decried the administration's rhetoric on Alex Pretti's gun. CNN Politics. https://www.cnn.com/2026/01/27/politics/gun-alex-pretti-ice-nra

13 NRA calling Essayli's comments "dangerous and wrong": NRA (@NRA). (2026, January 25). [Post on X]. Cited in: Newsweek. (2026, January 26). NRA makes rare statement against Trump admin over Alex Pretti shooting. Newsweek. https://www.newsweek.com/nra-makes-rare-statement-against-trump-admin-over-alex-pretti-shooting-11321317

14 Gun Owners of America on Second Amendment at protests: Axios. (2026, January 25). Gun rights groups challenge Minnesota shooting of Alex Pretti by Border Patrol. Axios. https://www.axios.com/2026/01/25/gun-groups-challenge-minneapolis-shooting-pretti

15 Minnesota Gun Owners Caucus statement: Axios. (2026, January 25). Gun rights groups challenge Minnesota shooting of Alex Pretti by Border Patrol. Axios. https://www.axios.com/2026/01/25/gun-groups-challenge-minneapolis-shooting-pretti

16 Massie statement: Washington Examiner. (2026, January 25). Massie says carrying gun not 'death sentence' after Pretti shooting. Washington Examiner. https://www.washingtonexaminer.com/news/justice/4432867/massie-gun-rights-minneapolis-pretti-shooting

17 NRA calling for full investigation; demonizing law-abiding citizens: Fox 9. (2026, January 25). NRA slams U.S. attorney's response to latest Minneapolis shooting. Fox 9 KMSP. https://www.fox9.com/news/nra-statements-minnesota-minneapolis-shooting-alex-pretti

18 Haidt moral foundations — convergence on fairness and liberty: Haidt, J. (2012). The righteous mind: Why good people are divided by politics and religion. Pantheon Books; Graham, J., Haidt, J., & Nosek,

B. A. (2009). Liberals and conservatives rely on different sets of moral foundations. Journal of Personality and Social Psychology, 96(5), 1029–1046. https://doi.org/10.1037/a0015141

19 Motivated discounting of cross-group defense: Kunda, Z. (1990). The case for motivated reasoning. Psychological Bulletin, 108(3), 480–498. https://doi.org/10.1037/0033-2909.108.3.480; Taber, C. S., & Lodge, M. (2006). Motivated skepticism in the evaluation of political beliefs. American Journal of Political Science, 50(3), 755–769. https://doi.org/10.1111/j.1540-5907.2006.00214.x

20 Opposition mobilizes; values sustain: Chenoweth, E., & Stephan, M. J. (2011). Why civil resistance works: The strategic logic of nonviolent conflict. Columbia University Press; Sherif, M., Harvey, O. J., White, B. J., Hood, W. R., & Sherif, C. W. (1961). Intergroup conflict and cooperation: The Robbers Cave experiment. University of Oklahoma Press.

Chapter 12 Reference Notes

1. PBS NewsHour. (2026, February 10). Walk for Peace concludes as Buddhist monks arrive in Washington after 15-week trek. PBS. https://www.pbs.org/newshour/nation/walk-for-peace-concludes-as-buddhist-monks-arrive-in-washington-after-15-week-trek

2. Walk for Peace. (2025, November). Wikipedia. https://en.wikipedia.org/wiki/Walk_for_Peace; NBC News. (2026, February 10). Buddhist monks' 15-week walk for peace ends in Washington, D.C. https://www.nbcnews.com/news/us-news/buddhist-monks-15-week-walk-peace-ends-washington-dc-rcna258458

3. Walk for Peace Wikipedia, supra note 2. Aloka's surgery on his cranial cruciate ligament (CCL) took place on January 12, 2026, at the Charleston Veterinary Referral Center.

4. KERA News. (2026, February 10). Watch Fort Worth monks arrive in Washington, DC. https://www.keranews.org/news/2026-02-10/watch-fort-worth-monks-arrive-in-washington-dc-walk-for-peace-enters-the-capital; Fox 5 DC. (2026, February 10). Monks "Walk for Peace" reaches DC. https://www.fox5dc.com/news/monks-walk-peace-set-arrive-dc-tuesday. The 20,000-plus livestream viewer figure is reported at the Lincoln Memorial concluding ceremony on February 11 and confirmed across multiple wire reports (AP; Washington Times, February 12, 2026).

5. NPR. (2026, February 11). These Buddhist monks' walk for peace captivated Americans. It ends this week. https://www.npr.org/2026/02/11/

nx-s1-5708853/these-monks-simple-walk-for-peace-captivated-millions-it-ends-this-week; Fort Worth Report. (2026, February 11). Walk for Peace Buddhist monks gather at Lincoln Memorial in DC for concluding ceremony. https://fortworthreport.org/2026/02/11/walk-for-peace-buddhist-monks-gather-at-lincoln-memorial-in-dc-for-concluding-ceremony/

6. Walk for Peace Wikipedia, supra note 2. Follower counts as of February 14, 2026.

7. Associated Press / NBC News, supra note 2. Long Si Dong quoted in multiple wire reports including PBS NewsHour (supra note 1) and the AP dispatch carried by NBC News.

8. Lerner, J. S., & Keltner, D. (2001). Fear, anger, and risk. Journal of Personality and Social Psychology, 81(1), 146–159; Kahneman, D. (2011). Thinking, fast and slow. Farrar, Straus and Giroux.

9. Kahneman, D. (2011). Thinking, fast and slow. Farrar, Straus and Giroux.

10. Brown, B. (2017). Braving the wilderness. Random House.

11. Brady, W. J., Wills, J. A., Jost, J. T., Tucker, J. A., & Van Bavel, J. J. (2017). Emotion shapes the diffusion of moralized content in social networks. Proceedings of the National Academy of Sciences, 114(28), 7313–7318. https://doi.org/10.1073/pnas.1618923114; Vosoughi, S., Roy, D., & Aral, S. (2018). The spread of true and false news online. Science, 359(6380), 1146–1151. https://doi.org/10.1126/science.aap9559

12. Chenoweth, E., & Stephan, M. J. (2011). Why civil resistance works: The strategic logic of nonviolent conflict. Columbia University Press. The 3.5 percent threshold is discussed extensively in secondary literature; see also Chenoweth, E. (2020). Questions, answers, and some cautionary updates regarding the 3.5% rule. Carr Center for Human Rights Policy, Harvard Kennedy School.

13. Crowd Counting Consortium. (2017–present). Crowd counting data. Harvard Kennedy School / University of Connecticut. https://ash.harvard.edu/programs/crowd-counting-consortium/; Chenoweth, E. et al. (2025, August 12). New data shows No Kings was one of the largest days of protest in US history. Waging Nonviolence. https://wagingnonviolence.org/2025/08/new-data-shows-no-kings-was-one-of-the-largest-days-of-protest-in-us-history/

14. NPR. (2025, June 17). The strategy behind nonviolent protest movement in the U.S. https://www.npr.org/2025/06/17/nx-s1-5435298/the-strategy-behind-nonviolent-protest-movement-in-the-u-s (quot-

ing Erica Chenoweth on the 99.5 percent nonviolence figure for the April–May 2025 period; the pattern continued through the No Kings demonstrations).

15. Britannica. (2025). No Kings protests. https://www.britannica.com/event/No-Kings-protests; Wikipedia. (2025). June 2025 No Kings protests. https://en.wikipedia.org/wiki/June_2025_No_Kings_protests; Wikipedia. (2025). October 2025 No Kings protests. https://en.wikipedia.org/wiki/October_2025_No_Kings_protests. Attendance estimates from organizers, ACLU, and Crowd Counting Consortium as reported across sources. The chapter uses organizer figures; independent CCC estimates place June turnout between 2 and 4.8 million and October turnout between 5 and 6.5 million.

16. Bridging Divides Initiative. (2026). Protest activity in the United States, 2025. Princeton University. https://bridgingdivides.princeton.edu

17. Kahneman, D. (2011). Thinking, fast and slow. Farrar, Straus and Giroux; Stanovich, K. E. (2009). What intelligence tests miss: The psychology of rational thought. Yale University Press.

18. Powell, C. (2003, February 5). Remarks to the United Nations Security Council. U.S. Department of State; Powell, C. (2005, September 8). Interview. ABC News / CBS News.

References

Associated Press. (2026, February 10). Buddhist monks' 15-week walk for peace ends in Washington, D.C. NBC News. https://www.nbcnews.com/news/us-news/buddhist-monks-15-week-walk-peace-ends-washington-dc-rcna258458

Al Jazeera. (2026, January 25). Who was Alex Pretti, the nurse shot dead by federal agents in Minneapolis? Al Jazeera. https://www.aljazeera.com/news/2026/1/25/who-was-alex-pretti-the-nurse-shot-dead-by-federal-agents-in-minneapolis

Axios. (2026, January 25). Gun rights groups challenge Minnesota shooting of Alex Pretti by Border Patrol. Axios. https://www.axios.com/2026/01/25/gun-groups-challenge-minneapolis-shooting-pretti

Brady, W. J., Wills, J. A., Jost, J. T., Tucker, J. A., & Van Bavel, J. J. (2017). Emotion shapes the diffusion of moralized content in social networks. Proceedings of the National Academy of Sciences, 114(28), 7313–7318. https://doi.org/10.1073/pnas.1618923114

Bridging Divides Initiative. (2026). Protest activity in the United States, 2025. Princeton University. https://bridgingdivides.princeton.edu

Britannica. (2025). No Kings protests. Encyclopaedia Britannica. https://www.britannica.com/event/No-Kings-protests

Brown, B. (2017). Braving the wilderness: The quest for true belonging and the courage to stand alone. Random House.

Burns, S. (2011). The Central Park Five: A chronicle of a city wilding. Knopf.

Burton, R. A. (2008). On being certain: Believing you are right even when you're not. St. Martin's Press.

CBS News. (2005, September 9). Powell calls U.N. speech "painful." CBS News. https://www.cbsnews.com/news/powell-calls-un-speech-painful/

CBS News. (2026, January 26). In Alex Pretti's killing, a sharp contrast between what Trump officials say and what video shows. CBS News. https://www.cbsnews.com/news/alex-pretti-shooting-contrast-official-accounts-videos

CBS News. (2026, January 28). Growing number of Republicans criticize Trump officials' response to Alex Pretti's shooting. CBS News. https://www.cbsnews.com/news/alex-pretti-shooting-minneapolis-growing-number-of-republicans-criticize-trump-admin-response

Chenoweth, E., Hammam, S., Pressman, J., & Shay, C. W. (2025, August 12). New data shows No Kings was one of the largest days of protest in US history. Waging Nonviolence. https://wagingnonviolence.org/2025/08/new-data-shows-no-kings-was-one-of-the-largest-days-of-protest-in-us-history/

Chenoweth, E., Hammam, S., Pressman, J., & Shay, C. W. (2025, October 16). The resistance reaches into Trump country. Waging Nonviolence. https://wagingnonviolence.org/2025/10/resistance-reaches-into-trump-counties/

Chenoweth, E., & Stephan, M. J. (2011). Why civil resistance works: The strategic logic of nonviolent conflict. Columbia University Press.

Cialdini, R. B. (1984). Influence: The psychology of persuasion. William Morrow.

Clark, A. (2013). Whatever next? Predictive brains, situated agents, and the future of cognitive science. Behavioral and Brain Sciences, 36(3), 181–204. https://doi.org/10.1017/S0140525X12000477

CNN. (2026, January 25). January 24, 2026 — Fatal shooting of Minneapolis man [Live updates]. CNN. https://www.cnn.com/us/live-news/ice-minneapolis-shooting-01-24-26

CNN. (2026, January 27). Gun-rights groups decried the administration's rhetoric on Alex Pretti's gun. CNN Politics. https://www.cnn.com/2026/01/27/politics/gun-alex-pretti-ice-nra

Crombag, H. F. M., Wagenaar, W. A., & van Koppen, P. J. (1996). Crashing memories and the problem of "source monitoring." Applied Cognitive Psychology, 10(2), 95–104. https://doi.org/10.1002/(SICI)1099-0720(199604)10:2<95::AID-ACP366>3.0.CO;2-#

Crowd Counting Consortium. (2017–present). Crowd counting data. Harvard Kennedy School / University of Connecticut. https://ash.harvard.edu/programs/crowd-counting-consortium/

Dechêne, A., Stahl, C., Hansen, J., & Wänke, M. (2010). The truth about the truth: A meta-analytic review of the truth effect. Personality and Social Psychology Review, 14(2), 238–257. https://doi.org/10.1177/1088868309352251

DeYoung, K. (2006). Soldier: The life of Colin Powell. Alfred A. Knopf.

Eligon, J. (2014, June 19). New York settles with Central Park Five for $41 million. The New York Times. https://www.nytimes.com/2014/06/19/nyregion/new-york-settles-with-central-park-five-for-41-million.html

Ellul, J. (1965). Propaganda: The formation of men's attitudes. Knopf.

Evans, J. St. B. T., Barston, J. L., & Pollard, P. (1983). On the conflict between logic and belief in syllogistic reasoning. Memory & Cognition, 11(3), 295–306. https://doi.org/10.3758/BF03196976

Fazio, L. K. (2020). Repetition increases perceived truth even for known falsehoods. Collabra: Psychology, 6(1), Article 38. https://doi.org/10.1525/collabra.347

Fazio, L. K., Brashier, N. M., Payne, B. K., & Marsh, E. J. (2015). Knowledge does not protect against illusory truth. Journal of Experimental Psychology: General, 144(5), 993–1002. https://doi.org/10.1037/xge0000098

Fort Worth Report. (2026, February 10). Thousands gather in DC for Fort Worth monks' Walk for Peace arrival. Fort Worth Report. https://fortworthreport.org/2026/02/10/fort-worth-buddhist-monks-arrive-in-washington-dc/

Fort Worth Report. (2026, February 11). Walk for Peace Buddhist monks gather at Lincoln Memorial in DC for concluding ceremony. Fort Worth Report. https://fortworthreport.org/2026/02/11/walk-for-peace-buddhist-monks-gather-at-lincoln-memorial-in-dc-for-concluding-ceremony/

Fox 9 KMSP. (2026, January 25). NRA slams U.S. attorney's response to latest Minneapolis shooting. Fox 9. https://www.fox9.com/news/nra-statements-minnesota-minneapolis-shooting-alex-pretti

Graham, J., Haidt, J., & Nosek, B. A. (2009). Liberals and conservatives rely on different sets of moral foundations. Journal of Personality and Social Psychology, 96(5), 1029–1046. https://doi.org/10.1037/a0015141

Haidt, J. (2012). The righteous mind: Why good people are divided by politics and religion. Pantheon Books.

Hasher, L., Goldstein, D., & Toppino, T. (1977). Frequency and the conference of referential validity. Journal of Verbal Learning and Verbal Behavior, 16(1), 107–112. https://doi.org/10.1016/S0022-5371(77)80012-1

Kahan, D. M. (2013). Ideology, motivated reasoning, and cognitive reflection. Judgment and Decision Making, 8(4), 407–424.

Kahan, D. M., Peters, E., Dawson, E., & Slovic, P. (2017). Motivated numeracy and enlightened self-government. Behavioural Public Policy, 1(1), 54–86. https://doi.org/10.1017/bpp.2016.2

Kahneman, D. (2011). Thinking, fast and slow. Farrar, Straus and Giroux.

Kassin, S. M. (2012). Why confessions trump innocence. American Psychologist, 67(6), 431–445. https://doi.org/10.1037/a0028212

KERA News. (2026, February 10). Watch Fort Worth monks arrive in Washington, DC, Walk for Peace enters the capital. KERA News. https://www.keranews.org/news/2026-02-10/watch-fort-worth-monks-arrive-in-washington-dc-walk-for-peace-enters-the-capital

Klein, G. (1998). Sources of power: How people make decisions. MIT Press.

Kunda, Z. (1990). The case for motivated reasoning. Psychological Bulletin, 108(3), 480–498. https://doi.org/10.1037/0033-2909.108.3.480

Lavietes, M., Melendez, P., Romero, D., & Stelloh, T. (2026, January 26). What we know about Alex Pretti, the ICU nurse killed in Minneapolis by federal officials. NBC News. https://www.nbcnews.com/news/us-news/alex-pretti-fatally-shot-federal-officers-minneapolis-identified-paren-rcna255758

Lerner, J. S., & Keltner, D. (2001). Fear, anger, and risk. Journal of Personality and Social Psychology, 81(1), 146–159. https://doi.org/10.1037/0022-3514.81.1.146

Linville, P. W., & Jones, E. E. (1980). Polarized appraisals of out-group members. Journal of Personality and Social Psychology, 38(5), 689–703. https://doi.org/10.1037/0022-3514.38.5.689

Marshall, B. J., & Warren, J. R. (1984). Unidentified curved bacilli in the stomach of patients with gastritis and peptic ulceration. The Lancet, 323(8390), 1311–1315. https://doi.org/10.1016/S0140-6736(84)91816-6

Milgram, S. (1963). Behavioral study of obedience. Journal of Abnormal and Social Psychology, 67(4), 371–378. https://doi.org/10.1037/h0040525

Miller, W. R., & Rollnick, S. (2012). Motivational interviewing: Helping people change (3rd ed.). Guilford Press.

Morris, G. E. (2025, October 18). Second "No Kings Day" protests the largest single-day political protest ever, with 5.0–6.5 million participants. Strength In Numbers. https://www.gelliottmorris.com/p/second-no-kings-day-protests-likely

Newsweek. (2026, January 26). NRA makes rare statement against Trump admin over Alex Pretti shooting. Newsweek. https://www.newsweek.com/nra-makes-rare-statement-against-trump-admin-over-alex-pretti-shooting-11321317

Nobel Assembly at the Karolinska Institute. (2005). The Nobel Prize in

Physiology or Medicine 2005: Barry J. Marshall and J. Robin Warren. Nobel Media AB. https://www.nobelprize.org/prizes/medicine/2005/summary/

NPR. (2025, June 17). The strategy behind nonviolent protest movement in the U.S. NPR. https://www.npr.org/2025/06/17/nx-s1-5435298/the-strategy-behind-nonviolent-protest-movement-in-the-u-s

NPR. (2026, February 10). Buddhist monks' 15-week walk for peace ends in Washington, D.C. NPR. https://www.npr.org/2026/02/10/g-s1-109416/buddhist-monks-finish-walk-for-peace

NPR. (2026, February 11). These Buddhist monks' walk for peace captivated Americans. It ends this week. NPR. https://www.npr.org/2026/02/11/nx-s1-5708853/these-monks-simple-walk-for-peace-captivated-millions-it-ends-this-week

Paulhus, D. L., & Williams, K. M. (2002). The Dark Triad of personality: Narcissism, Machiavellianism, and psychopathy. Journal of Research in Personality, 36(6), 556–563. https://doi.org/10.1016/S0092-6566(02)00505-6

PBS NewsHour. (2026, January 27). Killing of Alex Pretti scrambles Second Amendment politics for Trump. PBS NewsHour. https://www.pbs.org/newshour/politics/killing-of-alex-pretti-scrambles-second-amendment-politics-for-trump

PBS NewsHour. (2026, February 10). Walk for Peace concludes as Buddhist monks arrive in Washington after 15-week trek. PBS NewsHour. https://www.pbs.org/newshour/nation/walk-for-peace-concludes-as-buddhist-monks-arrive-in-washington-after-15-week-trek

Pennycook, G., Cannon, T. D., & Rand, D. G. (2018). Prior exposure increases perceived accuracy of fake news. Journal of Experimental Psychology: General, 147(12), 1865–1880. https://doi.org/10.1037/xge0000465

Petty, R. E., & Cacioppo, J. T. (1986). Communication and persuasion: Central and peripheral routes to attitude change. Springer-Verlag.

Powell, C. (2003, February 5). U.S. Secretary of State addresses the U.N. Security Council [Transcript]. George W. Bush White House Archives. https://georgewbush-whitehouse.archives.gov/news/releases/2003/02/20030205-1.html

Powell, C. (2005, September 8). Interview with Barbara Walters [Television broadcast]. ABC News.

Presidential Commission on the Space Shuttle Challenger Accident.

(1986). Report of the Presidential Commission on the Space Shuttle Challenger Accident. U.S. Government Printing Office.

Pronin, E., & Kugler, M. B. (2007). Valuing thoughts, ignoring behavior: The introspection illusion as a source of the bias blind spot. Journal of Experimental Social Psychology, 43(4), 565–578. https://doi.org/10.1016/j.jesp.2006.05.011

Pronin, E., Lin, D. Y., & Ross, L. (2002). The bias blind spot: Perceptions of bias in self versus others. Personality and Social Psychology Bulletin, 28(3), 369–381. https://doi.org/10.1177/0146167202286008

Reber, R., & Schwarz, N. (1999). Effects of perceptual fluency on judgments of truth. Consciousness and Cognition, 8(3), 338–342. https://doi.org/10.1006/ccog.1999.0386

Semmelweis, I. P. (1861). Die Ätiologie, der Begriff und die Prophylaxis des Kindbettfiebers. Hartleben.

Sherman, D. K., & Cohen, G. L. (2006). The psychology of self-defense: Self-affirmation theory. In M. P. Zanna (Ed.), Advances in experimental social psychology (Vol. 38, pp. 183–242). Academic Press. https://doi.org/10.1016/S0065-2601(06)38004-5

Sherif, M., Harvey, O. J., White, B. J., Hood, W. R., & Sherif, C. W. (1961). Intergroup conflict and cooperation: The Robbers Cave experiment. University of Oklahoma Press.

Slovic, P., Finucane, M. L., Peters, E., & MacGregor, D. G. (2002). The affect heuristic. In T. Gilovich, D. Griffin, & D. Kahneman (Eds.), Heuristics and biases: The psychology of intuitive judgment (pp. 397–420). Cambridge University Press.

Stafford, J., & Stern, M. (2026, January 25). The Trump administration is lying about gun rights and the death of Alex Pretti. Reason. https://reason.com/2026/01/25/the-trump-administration-is-lying-about-gun-rights-and-the-death-of-alex-pretti

Stanovich, K. E., & West, R. F. (2008). On the relative independence of thinking biases and cognitive ability. Journal of Personality and Social Psychology, 94(4), 672–695. https://doi.org/10.1037/0022-3514.94.4.672

Stanovich, K. E. (2009). What intelligence tests miss: The psychology of rational thought. Yale University Press.

Stanovich, K. E. (2011). Rationality and the reflective mind. Oxford University Press.

Starbird, K., Arif, A., & Wilson, T. (2019). Disinformation as collaborative work: Surfacing the participatory nature of strategic information operations. Proceedings of the ACM on Human-Computer Interaction, 3(CSCW), Article 127. https://doi.org/10.1145/3359229

Steele, C. M. (1988). The psychology of self-affirmation: Sustaining the integrity of the self. In L. Berkowitz (Ed.), Advances in experimental social psychology (Vol. 21, pp. 261–302). Academic Press.

Taber, C. S., & Lodge, M. (2006). Motivated skepticism in the evaluation of political beliefs. American Journal of Political Science, 50(3), 755–769. https://doi.org/10.1111/j.1540-5907.2006.00214.x

Tajfel, H., & Turner, J. C. (1979). An integrative theory of intergroup conflict. In W. G. Austin & S. Worchel (Eds.), The social psychology of intergroup relations (pp. 33–47). Brooks/Cole.

Tangney, J. P. (1991). Moral affect: The good, the bad, and the ugly. Journal of Personality and Social Psychology, 61(4), 598–607. https://doi.org/10.1037/0022-3514.61.4.598

Tangney, J. P., & Dearing, R. L. (2002). Shame and guilt. Guilford Press.

Tetlock, P. E. (2005). Expert political judgment: How good is it? How can we know? Princeton University Press.

Tversky, A., & Kahneman, D. (1974). Judgment under uncertainty: Heuristics and biases. Science, 185(4157), 1124–1131. https://doi.org/10.1126/science.185.4157.1124

Vaughan, D. (1996). The Challenger launch decision: Risky technology, culture, and deviance at NASA. University of Chicago Press.

Vosoughi, S., Roy, D., & Aral, S. (2018). The spread of true and false news online. Science, 359(6380), 1146–1151. https://doi.org/10.1126/science.aap9559

Walk for Peace. (2025–2026). Wikipedia. https://en.wikipedia.org/wiki/Walk_for_Peace

Washington Examiner. (2026, January 25). Massie says carrying gun not 'death sentence' after Pretti shooting. Washington Examiner. https://www.washingtonexaminer.com/news/justice/4432867/massie-gun-rights-minneapolis-pretti-shooting

Washington Times. (2026, February 12). Thousands show at Lincoln Memorial for final day of Buddhist monks' 15-week journey from Texas. Washington Times. https://www.washingtontimes.com/news/2026/feb/12/thousands-show-lincoln-memorial-final-day-buddhist-monks-15-week/

Westen, D., Blagov, P. S., Harenski, K., Kilts, C., & Hamann, S. (2006).

REFERENCES

Neural bases of motivated reasoning: An fMRI study of emotional constraints on partisan political judgment in the 2004 U.S. presidential election. Journal of Cognitive Neuroscience, 18(11), 1947–1958. https://doi.org/10.1162/jocn.2006.18.11.1947

Wikipedia. (2025). June 2025 No Kings protests. https://en.wikipedia.org/wiki/June_2025_No_Kings_protests

Wikipedia. (2025). October 2025 No Kings protests. https://en.wikipedia.org/wiki/October_2025_No_Kings_protests

Wikipedia. (2026). Killing of Alex Pretti. https://en.wikipedia.org/wiki/Killing_of_Alex_Pretti

Wylie, C. (2019). Mindf*ck: Cambridge Analytica and the plot to break America. Random House.

ABOUT THE AUTHOR

W. B. Hazel

W. B. Hazel has a bachelor of science degree in Biology from the University of Idaho with minors in Botany and Zoology.

She owns and operates Fishing Frog Print House, a boutique publishing business in Boise, Idaho. She is an avid outdoor enthusiast who can be found fishing, hiking, camping and huckleberry picking on her days off.

Fishing Frog Print House specializes in medium and high content nonfiction books.

www.ingramcontent.com/pod-product-compliance
Lightning Source LLC
LaVergne TN
LVHW040223110826
845146LV00004B/1260

* 9 7 9 8 9 9 5 5 9 1 5 1 1 *